What others are saying about "Keep Your Sanity and Your Shirt":

"The instructions given by Rita made it simple and easy to set up our business. It felt reassuring to be able to do it on our own. Being first time business owners there was a lot that we didn't know. (We also found a lot of people that didn't give us the right answers.) Rita's knowledge was very helpful since we were able to ask her the hard questions. We were comfortable with her way of working and her enthusiasm. I highly recommend this book to everyone who is starting a business and those who are running one. Thanks a million Rita."

Tania & Shawn Scott

Hey mom, I've read through the book and I am duly impressed. This is valuable information in a very accessible format. Awesome!!! Good luck with the launch. I can see why normal people with small businesses would find it to be a valuable resource.

Steven Fipke
Petroleum Engineer/ Business Unit Manager
Maturin, Venezuela, South America

Thanks to the work Rita has done, I have entered the corporate world without the hassle of learning the confusing new language, expensive lawyers and accountants. Rita's many years of creating and operating businesses, has made her an expert at eliminating the unneeded fluff that confuses and intimidates the rest of us. Simple directions and easy to understand story's, make Rita's perspective on business refreshing and most of all, attainable. Thanks for your guidance on this path of my journey!

Sandra Greene, small business owner

Alberta Edition

Keep Your Sanity
and Your Shirt

*A No-Pain Guide to
Small Business Start Up and Incorporation*

**Rita Fipke
Janet MacLeod**

KEEP YOUR SANITY AND YOUR SHIRT

To my children, Steven and Lynelle,
and my husband, Ron,
without whose constant support and encouragement,
this book would not have been possible.

And to Peter and Laura Graham
for your proofreading and
all the support you've given me.

~Rita

To: Mummy. (She likes when I write stuff.)

~Janet

TABLE OF CONTENTS

Introduction 1

Chapter 1: Is Going "Corporate" Right For You? 3

Chapter 2: Naming Your Company 13

Chapter 3: Corporate Structure .19

Chapter 4: Registering Your Company 27

Chapter 5: GST: When, How and Where? 37

Chapter 6: Tax Matters and Your Accountant 45

Chapter 7: Running Your Business As a Business 67

Chapter 8: Paying Yourself:
Getting $$ Out of Your Corporation 73

Chapter 9: Employees and Payroll 77

About the Authors 81

Worth Investigating 85

Bibliography 87

Appendices 89

INTRODUCTION

During the thirty years spent following my wonderful husband, Ron, around the oil patch, we started and managed three different oilfield service companies as partnerships. We learned a great deal from those experiences: from accountants, lawyers, courses, and just plain old trial and error. In the beginning, I was the type of person who "supported"—doing books and administrative tasks. I didn't want to be bothered with the planning aspects, but Ron kept saying that one of us had to start paying attention to our personal financial situation: our investments and retirement plan, etc. Being independent consultants, we didn't have this "taken care of" by an employer. No one else had as vested an interest as we did, and Ron just didn't have the time to take on the responsibility, so, with some trepidation, I began. My formal corporate education started with a weekend seminar on managing your money and how millionaires think, where I discovered a new world of doing business (as a corporation) and, as a nice bonus, quite a bit about pro-active money management! I remember thinking, "Oh, this isn't so hard! This can be fun!" Suddenly I wanted to know. I started exploring possibilities, learning, taking more courses, and seeing what worked for us. I was unstoppable and having a great time doing it. Soon, friends started asking me for help, and I found myself consulting, helping people set up and manage their businesses more and more. People liked what was happening. They found my advice simple, practical and, most importantly, successful and kept encouraging me to write this down so others could benefit from it.

I toyed with the idea for a long time, but was intimidated by the sheer size of the undertaking. Enter Janet. She came to the project with a number of years of writing experience and agreed to help with that aspect of the book. She is the wordsmith of this whole venture!

So here we are…..

Everything you never really wanted to know-- but needed to know anyway-- about incorporating and running a business….successfully!

We will endeavor to keep things simple, while making them as fun and pleasant as possible. Just to warn you, though, we have interspersed some humor throughout the book, for which we'll ask your indulgence. We found it wildly amusing and made the writing of the book considerably more fun. We hope you enjoy it too and if not, please rest assured that it doesn't affect the accuracy of anything.

The chapters are not only designed to flow into and guide you through business set up and management, but for ease of reference. We want you to be an amazing success!! Statistics claim that only *one out of three* small business start-ups actually make it past five years…*we want you to be that one*!!!

CHAPTER 1

IS GOING "CORPORATE" RIGHT FOR YOU?

Sole Proprietorships/Partnership:

Most people start out as either a sole proprietor or within a partnership. The only difference between the two is that a sole proprietor, as the name implies, is one person, whereas a partnership can entail two or more (you and your spouse/ your best friend/ your daughter/ whomever). This is the simplest and most common form of small business. You're doing the business by yourselves. You are your business. Everything is all mixed and inter-mingled. When you get paid for business stuff, it goes into your personal pocket and you are taxed at personal tax rates.

As a sole proprietor- *YOU are fully responsible for all debts and obligations related to your business.*

Advantages

- relatively low start-up costs;
- greatest freedom from regulation;
- owner is in direct control of decision making;
- minimal working capital required;
- tax advantages to owner; business expenses are claimed on personal tax.

Disadvantages

• unlimited liability – you are personally (financially) responsible for everything involving your business--including the liability involved should someone decide to sue you because of something your business did, did not do, or should have done;
• lack of continuity in business organization during times of owner absence;
• difficulty raising capital – banks and other lending institutes don't really want to talk to you;
• all profits must be declared by the owner and are therefore taxed at the higher "personal" tax rates.

Maintaining a sole proprietorship can be beneficial at tax time during your business start-up. Should your business make virtually no money (or even, Heaven forbid, operate at a loss) it's in your best interests (tax wise) to remain a sole proprietor as you may claim those business expenses/losses against your employment income (if, for example, you are still working elsewhere and getting a T-4 at year end). This reduces your personal income and therefore, the amount of tax you pay. For example, should you decide to start up Business ZYX in April of 2005, but you worked for an employer up to that point in time (and thus, paid tax) you can claim your new business's loss against that employment income and get some, if not all, of your taxes back. This also works in the case of a husband/wife partnership where they are 50/50 partners in a new business with, for example, the husband working full time for an employer and supplying what-ever capital the wife's new business requires, then the husband may claim 50% of the business's loss against HIS employment income.

Keep Your Sanity and Your Shirt

Setting up a sole proprietorship:

Doesn't take very much-- it's virtually a *no brainer*. In fact, if you're doing business by yourself at this moment, you are considered a sole proprietor. Should you choose to name your business, the easiest way to do so is to visit your bank where they will search and register your chosen name for a nominal fee at the same time as you set up your separate bank account.

A tidbit from Rita:
A separate bank account, even if it's not a 'business' account, is a wise idea. It helps to keep things organized, and is especially helpful at tax time.

In a nutshell, a sole proprietorship is great when you're not making money. When you do start to make money (and you will, because we believe in you), then we need to talk incorporation....

Corporations:

This is where I come in...

"A corporation is a legal entity that is separate from its owners, the shareholders. No shareholder of a corporation is personally liable for the debts, obligations or acts of the corporation."
(Source: cbsc.org/alberta "Corporate Registry Services")

Is Going "Corporate" Right For You?
5

What does this really mean?

It means that you and your corporation are two separate entities. The business has an identity, like a person. It can be bought, sold or willed and you cannot be held totally liable for its actions... kind of like having a teenager. We'll discuss how you can be held liable later.

A corporation is identified by the following words and their abbreviations: "Limited", "Ltd.", "Incorporated", "Inc.", "Corporation", or "Corp.". Whatever the term, the corporate name must appear somewhere on all documents (stationery, invoices, and so on) in the same manner as it appears on the incorporation document. Thus, if you're called the **XYZ Corporation** on your incorporation document, you must be called **XYZ Corporation** on your stationery; however, you'll sometimes see a name like *"Fipke Electric: a division of 123456 Alberta Ltd."* where the latter half of the name is in small print. Alternatively, Fipke Electric may be used as the Trade Name for 123456 Alberta Ltd. In that case, Joe Blipke can run his business or store as Fipke Electric or as Fipke Electric a division of 123456 Alberta Ltd. *Apologies to anyone owning 123456 Alberta Limited. No reference is intended.*

Advantages:

• limited liability;
• specialized management: has officers, directors, etc;
• ownership is transferable and saleable;
• continuous existence: can be willed to heirs;
• separate legal entity;
• possible tax advantages: small business tax credits, lower taxation rates;
• easier to raise capital (the banks are more willing to talk to you now)

Disadvantages:

- closely regulated – you do have some rules to follow
- historically, the most expensive form to organize—until now!!
- charter restrictions;
- double taxation of dividends;
- possible development of conflict between shareholders – discuss the divorce up front!
- necessary record keeping – you should be keeping some kind of records anyway!

Corporation Type

The most common form of corporation consists of yourself, your spouse and/or a friend who is now your business partner. There are three types of corporations, which may be formed:

1. Corporations with 15 or less shareholders - these are the most common corporations in Alberta and have the least amount of regulation.

2. Corporations with 16 or more shareholders, which do not let the general public have any shares - these corporations must prepare shareholders' lists for meetings and comply with various sections of the Business Corporations Act.

3. Corporations with 16 or more shareholders, which do distribute shares to the public - this type of corporation is subject to the most regulation. It must file financial statements and other documentation with the Alberta Securities Commission.

So, what does this mean to the average person? It means that you can be a corporation as a single person or as many people. As a single person, you will be the only shareholder and director of the corporation, thereby making unanimous corporate decisions extremely easy (at least, we hope so).

A corporation of many people necessitates a partnership agreement. A partnership agreement is a written contract setting out the terms of the partnership: how many shares each partner owns, who does what, who invests what into the company, and the divorce structure— meaning how will the partnership be dissolved. There will come a time when the partnership/love affair will end. How will the divorce be structured? Who gets what and how? Talking about it up front makes it so much easier. If the partnership is with anyone but your spouse, it's a very good idea to have a lawyer draw up the agreement.

Tax benefits

Small business deduction is a special tax rate that qualifying Canadian Controlled Private Corporations (CCPC's) get charged. You qualify as a CCPC if at least 50% of your shares are owned by Canadians and at least 50% of your directors are residents of Canada. This small business deduction _reduces_ the tax rate to about 17-22% on the first $200,000.00 of taxable income: meaning, the profits made by your corporation after all your expenses are taken out! The _normal_ corporate tax rate (before the reduction) is 50% - a huge savings!!

Since a corporation has this lower tax rate – being _approximately_ 20% on the first $200,000 of the corporation's taxable income (depending on current taxation laws), it's just a smarter option. Compare corporate rate with being taxed at your personal rate for all of your business' income if you operate as a sole proprietor (generally starting at around 35 % and rising from there!).

The corporation would pay tax in the neighbourhood of $40,000 on $200,000 of profit made. The sole proprietor? A whole lot more, between $80- $100,000. *Quite the difference!!*

The corporate structure also allows greater flexibility and opportunities as to how you pay yourself, thereby reducing personal income taxes—it allows for income sharing with other family members (saving more taxes) and for deferring taxes into the future years. These and a few other benefits make being corporate very attractive when you are doing your tax planning... and we want all the help we can get when it comes to taxes!!

Disadvantages:

- The hassle of doing the registration – we are here to help make it easier...
- You have to keep a minute book - we will show you how.
- You have to file corporate returns once a year (in effect, pay for the honour of doing business for another year, while informing the government of your intent to do so.)
- You have to do a corporate year-end. And, unless your alter ego is "Number Man", an accountant has to do this-- and your tax return-- for you.

All of these can be easy to do if you know how!

So, you've decided to form a 'limited' corporation....

How is a limited corporation formed? To form a limited corporation, you must decide on and provide a name for your company/ corporation, provide an address, describe the **structure** of your company (meaning who owns it and who has shares in it), and who are the corporate directors.

Private Corporation

(most common corporate form, and probably what you will be doing)

The word 'limited' at the end of a Canadian corporation's name implies that liability of the corporation's shareholders is limited to the money they paid to buy the shares. By contrast, ownership by sole proprietor or partnership carries unlimited personal legal responsibility for debts incurred by the business. Meaning, if you're a sole proprietor and your business owes someone some money or service, and the business goes under, YOU are still responsible. If you are a corporation, however, your liability is limited.

(Source: "Incorporating and Organizing a Corporation",
The Legal Ease Library Inc.,2002: Calgary, Alberta)

As discussed earlier, incorporation separates you from your business, although often if you are borrowing money the bank will make you sign a "Personal guarantee" that you will make good any money they might be loaning your corporation. In effect, the bank wants your assurance that you will stand behind the debt. This is the only liability that can be placed on you personally.

A tidbit from Rita:

At the start up of a corporation, people often put in their own personal money and assets. Should you do this, you then become a creditor to the corporation, and it owes you the value of these assets. This means it has to pay you back, so you now have a shareholders loan that will appear as a debt on the company balance sheet. You can choose to have this repaid at any time that is mutually beneficial to you and the corporation-- your accountant can help you to decide when.

A word on liability from *the Government of Canada Web site*:

Total business liabilities

A liability is a debt or obligation of a business. Total business liabilities are the total of all amounts your business or professional activity owes at the end of its fiscal period. This includes:

• accounts payable;
• notes payable;
• taxes payable;
• unpaid salaries, wages, and benefits;
• interest payable;
• deferred or unearned revenues;
• loans payable;
• mortgages payable; and any other outstanding balance related to the business

What are my Corporate Liabilities?

Okay. Corporate shareholders are generally exempt from liability **except** for wages owed or in cases where they've signed a personal guarantee to a lender (usually a bank). Should your company go bankrupt, or amass huge debt, assets will be sold off to pay as much as possible of the unpaid debt but you are not personally responsible to any creditors. As a director of the corporation, it's not only your job, but also your duty to act in the best interests of the company. Meaning, you act with honesty, integrity and responsibility in all affairs of business.

You can be held personally liable for up to six months of corporate employee's wages, unpaid corporate taxes or tax violations, and/or any illegal or unscrupulous actions involving company funds.

CHAPTER 2

NAMING YOUR COMPANY

Corporate Names

There are different types of names. You can have a "named" name, such as ABC Holdings Ltd., or a "numbered" name, such as 123456 Alberta Ltd.

Legal Elements

www.ccra.gc.ca is a great website with a positive plethora of pertinent information. It is, unfortunately, written in government-eze. *We feel for you, really, but stay with us here. You really do want to read this...*

A "named" name should consist of three parts, or elements. The first part is usually the distinctive element. In the example, "ABC Holdings Ltd.", the distinctive element is "ABC". This part should set your name apart from other names, making it easy to remember. The second part describes what the corporation does or is. In our example, "Holdings" is the descriptive element. The third part is the legal element - our legal element in this case is "Ltd." There are other legal elements, one of which must be in your corporation's name. Accepted legal elements are:
* *Limited*
* *Limitee*
* *Ltee*
* *Ltd.*
* *Corp.*

- *Corporation*
- *Inc.*
- *Incorporated*
- *Incorporee*

Professional Corporations Another type of "named" name corporation is a "Professional Corporation" which is a corporation specifically formed for one of the following types of professions:
- *law*
- *medicine*
- *dentistry*
- *optometry*
- *chiropractic*
- *chartered accountant*
- *certified management accountant*
- *certified general accountant*

This type of corporation will have the person's name, followed by the term "Professional Corporation". An example of a professional corporation's name would be "John Smith Professional Corporation".

Step 1: Reserving a Name

You get to have some fun choosing what your company will be called, but remember, this is often your customer's first take on your business. How do you want the world to view you? Will your company name give your target audience – your customers and clients-- an idea of what it is you are selling? Does it say what your company is or what your company does? Does the name encourage people to ask for more information, giving you a thirty second marketing opportunity-- for free?

Very often, people will name their company something non-descriptive like R & R Enterprises. Unfortunately, while R & R Enterprises may do counseling, there is nothing in the name to reflect that. It is a perfectly legal, "accountant-y" type name, but it does not sell the product or service.

A tidbit from Rita:

Bottom line is: we are all selling something-- be it a product or a service. Why not let your name do some of the marketing for you?

It has been said that naming your corporation is more difficult than naming your children and definitely has greater repercussions.

(Source: Incorporating and Organizing a Corporation)

Once you've decided on a business name, you can reserve said name by filing a declaration form-- a key component in the registration process. The form asks you to provide basic information about the company and its owner.

(a) the company's type
(b) the company's name and address
(c) the owner's name and occupation
(d) the company's starting date
(e) the name of the officer authorizing the declaration

A sample form can be viewed online by visiting: www3.gov.ab.ca/gs/information/publications/forms_tradename.cfm or by visiting any corporate registry office (the same place you register your car).

(Warning: Much legal jargon to follow! Coffee may be needed here.)

Registering a trade name in Alberta does not mean that you own that name. Many sole proprietorships in the province operate with duplicate names, as there is no requirement under the Partnership Act for a business name to be unique. As well, Alberta Registries has no obligation to avoid name duplication or to advise anyone registering a name that has been previously registered.

Corporations, on the other hand, must choose a unique name. Alberta Registries (www.plates.net/CorporateRegistry), can perform a NUANS search that will provide you with a list of businesses with similar names.

Nuans Reports NUANS report for a "named" name is required to ensure that no one else has the identical name. If the report shows similar names, you will have to decide if the name you want is too close to the other names listed on the NUANS report. These other businesses may feel very strongly about you using a name similar to theirs and they do have the right to object to the Registrar of Corporations. The Registrar can force you to change the name of your corporation, so pick your name carefully. Alternately, the other company may have incurred debts or have an undesirable reputation that you may not want your customers to associate to your company. For further information, please refer to the Business Corporations Act and Regulations for rules on Corporate Names.

The NUANS Report is submitted to an accredited service provider at the time of incorporation and must be less than 91 days old and contain all 6 pages.

"Numbered" Names

A "numbered" name is also comprised of three parts - the numbered part, which is assigned by Corporate Registry, the word "Alberta", and your choice of one of the legal elements. A NUANS report is not necessary for a numbered name.

To incorporate with a "numbered" name, you must specifically request this type of name through the authorized service provider that you have selected.

Step 2: Authorization

Once the incorporation name form is filled out, it must be filed with an authorized service provider (again, this is the same place where you get your car registration done).

Authorized service providers perform the majority of Corporate Registry services. These are private sector firms that have been authorized by the government to offer some or most Corporate Registry services. An authorized service provider can be a registry agent office (the car registration place), a law firm, an accounting firm, or a search house.

Prior to obtaining any Corporate Registry service, you should discuss fees, payment options and filing requirements with your chosen authorized service provider (they'll have a funky sign on the wall saying they are an "authorized service provider--*accept no substitutions!*"☺ It is advisable to shop around for the best value for your money since fees are not regulated by the government and may vary from office to office.

For your convenience, a list of qualified registry agents and their office locations is available online for each of four service levels. The Government fees for services provided through the registry agent network can be found in the Registry Agent's Product Catalogue. www3.gov.ab.ca/gs/information/registries/fees/Product_Catalogue.pdf

Service providers are authorized to charge a service fee in addition to the government fee for the examination of your documents and the entry of these documents into the Corporate Registry database.

A listing of authorized service providers can be found in Alberta's Corporate Registry by visiting www3.gov.ab.ca/gs/services/cpnc/index.cfm or by consulting your local yellow pages directory.

Step 3: Filing Fees

According to the January 18, 2005 registry agent product catalogue published by the Government of Alberta, the government charge for incorporation is $100.00, but the authorized service provider can charge additional fees that may boost the cost anywhere from $300 to $500.

The government fee to register a partnership or limited partnerships is $50. Sole proprietorships require trade name registration only, with a government fee of $50. Again, remember that fees charged by private sector firms are not government regulated. Shop around for the best price. Make sure that the service provider is authorized (there will be a sign in the window or on the door stating this) and the fee is reasonable for your area.

Partnership and trade name searches cost $1 – but the agency sets the service fee. They can charge whatever their little hearts desire. Once again, shop around and ask questions. For more information, call "The Business Link" at 1-800-272-9675.

CHAPTER 3

CORPORATE STRUCTURE

The corporate entity is a separate legal entity (like a person) that has the capacity, rights, powers and privileges of a real person like you; therefore a corporation can do anything that a person can, as long as it is legal. Although you own the corporation, you must think of it as a completely separate legal entity – you are not the corporation, and the corporation is NOT you!! Also, as a shareholder, you do not own any of the assets of the corporation—it owns its own stuff.

A tidbit from Rita:

If XYZ Corporation sells vitamins-- and you use the vitamins it sells – you as a shareholder must buy them from the company. It is stealing if you take them and don't pay for them. At the very least, keep track of the amount you use and record them as shareholder's benefits.

Also, when XYZ Corporation makes money, the funds cannot go directly into your pocket. That is stealing, also. Any money coming in has to be recorded and deposited into the corporate bank account. There are strict laws under Revenue Canada's 'Income Tax Act' and the scary accountants that work there can and will impose stiff penalties and fines which are a pain in the you-know-what. Seeing as you, quite reasonably, don't want to have to deal with said scary people, keep XYZ's money in XYZ's pocket and everything will be fine.

Corporate structure:

You can, and most likely will, be all of the following:

Shareholders
The first hat you will wear in your new corporation. Shareholders are the owners of said corporation. They control corporate business by appointing directors-- for one-year terms-- to manage the corporation's business. The directors' primary objective is to make the corporation profitable and increase the company's value. When those objectives are reached, dividends can be declared and shareholders are paid. Shareholders do not personally manage the business.

Directors
Director/Directors are the policy makers of the corporation. They decide where the corporation is going, where it will borrow $$$-- if necessary—and they set out guidelines and provide advice to the *officers*. Directors must be eighteen years of age, not currently bankrupt, have normal mental capacity and consent to being a director. At least half of your directors must be residents of Canada. The names and address of the directors must be filed with the corporate registry at the time of incorporation. Changes made to the directorship must be filed within fifteen days of each change. The director is liable for up to six months of wages to the corporation's employees, and any taxes to be paid or remitted to the government. Coverage of directors by Workman's compensation board is optional and they are not entitled to benefits if they chose not to be covered. Directors appoint officers for indefinite terms.

Officers
Officers run the day-to-day operations of the corporation. They appoint managers, hire employees, etc. and generally manage the corporation as set out by the Directors.

Another tidbit from Rita:
In the beginning, as you set up your corporation, you may be a one-person show and wear all the hats. Should you choose to, you may also appoint other people to be on your team – for example, a director who helps with decision-making and policy for the corporation. You can easily adapt and change your corporate structure to fit your own situation.

What are shares?

Shares are units of ownership, which are issued to the people who are creating or buying into the business. Shareholders have the right to vote on corporate business, the right to receive declared dividends, and the right to receive the remaining assets of the corporation upon corporate dissolution (if the corporation dies or in the case of partnership divorce).

Shares are divided into different classes, so that you can decide on various rights of shareholders. Each share in each class has the same rights, but rights are exercised in proportion to the percentage of shares held by each person.

For example, if Janet has fifty-three shares and Sue has forty-seven of the same 100 class shares, Janet will receive 53% of the dividend declared and Sue will receive 47% of it.

There are:
• Class A shares, which have all rights.
• Class B shares, which have all rights.
(Class A and B shares are the same. The difference is in who is issued dividends at year-end)

- Class C shares, which have no right to vote, but have the other rights.
- Class D shares, which have no right to vote, but have the other rights.

(Class C and D shares are the same. The difference, again, is in how dividends will be issued at year-end.)

- Class E shares – non-voting preferred shares with special rights and restrictions. (These are for if/when you want to transfer assets into the corporation.)

For more information on share classes, see Section 85 of the income tax act, go online at
http://www.cra-arc.gc.ca/E/pub/tp/ic76-19r3/ic76-19r3-e.html

 or speak with your accountant.

It is not necessary to have all of these different types of share classes, but we've included them here for your information. Utilizing different classes as your company grows and becomes more successful can give you greater maneuverability.

Rita Says...

It is often a good idea when there are two partners (especially husband and wife); to set it up so that one partner owns 50% of 'A' shares and the other owns 50% of 'E' shares. This will give you the greatest amount of maneuverability in paying yourselves.

Issuing shares

It is most common for a new corporation to issue 100 shares at $.10 per share to its shareholders. At start up, your corporation has no value, but some money must be paid for the shares and ten cents has become the usual amount. This money (ten dollars) is then put into the corporate bank account. It is not necessary to pay large amounts of money for the start up shares to inject $$ into the corporation as it's actually most advantageous to pay the nominal amount and put the $$ in as shareholders' loans. (Speak to an accountant to make sure this fits with your business.)

If you are a married or in a common-law partnership there are significant tax advantages with income splitting if you set up your share structure to have one of you owning 50% of the 'A' shares and the other partner owning 50% of the 'E' shares. By doing it this way, you can draw shareholder's dividends or management fees (depending upon current tax laws) in equal amounts, thereby dividing your taxable income in two.

Rita says... here's something to crow about:

Let's say my husband Ron makes $200,000/year for consulting. If taxed as a private individual, Ron would be paying upwards of 55% in personal income tax. As a corporation, Ron makes "nothing". The corporation makes $200,000, Ron takes dividends of $40,000 and pays approximately $1000.00 in personal tax. Rita takes the same and pays the same.

The remaining $100,000 is left in the company to be used for incredibly outlandish and extravagant corporate business expenses like phone or company health care or fuel or computers or rent or vehicle payments or business training or business travel or whatever. In effect, the corporation pays a significant portion of allowable, taxable, everyday expenses, and Ron's tax rate reduces from 55% to the minimum base tax rate. This year, the accountant tells us we averaged 12%!! YAY!!

**Remember to speak with your accountant to get the current details of how this works as it changes each time there are changes made to tax laws.

Directors' and shareholders' meetings

Now that your corporation is formed, from time to time the directors and shareholders will be required to make certain decisions, which need to be recorded and documented. At these times you do not have to hold a formal meeting. Instead, a resolution can be written up and signed by all the directors or shareholders, depending upon your corporate structure. For example, as you are very busy running your business, you may not have the time for a meeting-- or you may just hate them-- and decide to have an informal discussion around the lunch table or at a coffee break instead. Once everything is decided, the appropriate action can be taken and the resolutions inserted into the *minute book*, thereby complying with corporate law.

Additional Information

When you form your corporation, you must tell the accredited service provider (the place where you register your car) where the corporation-- you-- are located (registered office) and where you want the corporation's mail to go (mailing address) if this address is different. You will also be required to submit the names, addresses, and Canadian residency status of your directors. This is the government's way of ensuring they know how to contact you and that Attila the Hun's scarier brother doesn't incorporate in Alberta.

Where do I go to incorporate?

Once you have gathered all of your information and required documentation, you must take it to an authorized service provider (in case you've forgotten, this is the place where you register your car). The "**authorized service provider**" will examine your information, and if it meets the current legislated requirements, will process the request and issue you a certificate of incorporation as proof that the registration has occurred. (This pretty piece of paper then goes in your **minute book.**)

More information is available online at http://www.gov.ab.ca/gs.

Now that you are the proud owner of a limited corporation and are President, Secretary, Treasurer or Director, Officer (and / or all of the above) you have some responsibilities:

Annual corporate returns must be filed with the government. This document lets the government know that you plan on doing business for another year and it costs you money to let them know. It will arrive in the mail on or around the corporation's anniversary and you can pay - usually around $20 at the "place you register your car" (**Registry Office**).

If you go through an accountant or lawyer, it can cost you from $50 - $300 and they don't do anything more than you could do. They just watch you sign the form and send it in (quite possibly) to the place where you register your car, or to the appropriate government office.

A minute book is a three ring binder (usually black – just because) in which you keep all the incorporation documents. Your yearly share-holder's meetings and/or any changes that are made legally to the company have to be recorded and filed in this book. It becomes the historical records of your company.

A Corporate Seal is a funky little tool that embosses legal documents with the corporation's name. By Albertan law, it is no longer mandatory to seal corporate documents and although some banks may ask for it, they'll usually abandon the notion if challenged.

Yearly Shareholders' Meetings

You must hold this meeting each year and fill out the form for the government that says you are going to do business for another year, to elect directors, appoint an accountant to do your year end books, and update any information that may have changed over the past year in your little black book – "The Minute Book". Then any changes have to be filed with your Annual Corporate returns.

If you are a corporation of you, or you and a spouse; this is often done over the breakfast table... 'Honey, do we want to continue business for another year? Shall we have "Accountant man" do our year-end books again? Are we still the directors, officers and shareholders?? Just checking! And you have had an Annual General Meeting!!!

Fill in the paper work, which is very simple, and mail it off.

It used be considered an appropriate practice to hold these meetings somewhere quiet, in solitude, so the officers could brainstorm and think...say Hawaii, Mexico, etc. As of the last few years, auditor Man, and Canada Customs and Revenue frowns on such practices, especially for us small businesses.

Taxes, another of your responsibilities, will be discussed in a later chapter. We're bettin' you're glued to the edge of your seat in anticipation.....

CHAPTER 4

REGISTERING YOUR COMPANY

Logistics/forms/where-to-go's and how-to's... the boring stuff

***Please note: unless otherwise stated, all of the following information can be found at*: http://www.cra-arc.gc.ca*

This is where you actually do the work: fill out the form and take it to the place where you register your car.

How to register for incorporation and for a Business Number

Once you've registered your corporation, you'll receive a business number, which will identify you from this moment forward, in all your dealings with the CCRA.

You can register for one or more Canada Revenue Agency (CRA) accounts at the same time. If you are incorporated and do not know your Business Number, contact your local Canada Revenue Agency office at 1-800-959-5525. To register for a business number or a CRA program account (i.e. GST), call, toll-free, 1-800-959-5525.

After the CRA mails confirmation of this Business Number (usually within five days), businesses can use it to register for other CRA programs (e.g.: GST/HST, Business Name, Workers' Compensation).

If you want to find the address of the closest tax services offices to your home or business, visit the Web site www.cra-arc.gc.ca or call 1-800-959-5525.
Hours of service are: weekdays from 8:15 am to 8:00 pm (local time)

To print business registration forms, visit the Web site
http://www.cra-arc.gc.ca/E/pbg/tf/rc1/README.html
If you prefer, you can order them the old fashioned way: toll-free at 1- 800- 959-2221.
Hours of service: weekdays from 8:00 am to 5:00 pm (Eastern Time)

Once you complete the form, submit it (mail, fax, or visit) to any Tax Services Office listed at www.cra-arc.gc.ca/contact/tso-e.html

Once you receive your notice of confirmation via Canada Post, you will be requested to mail a copy of your articles of incorporation (these are the papers you received after you visited the place where you register your car). Send these to the address provided on your notice.

Another tidbit from Rita:

Please don't send your originals!! If they get lost, they can be difficult to replace!!

For your convenience and ultimate viewing pleasure, we've included the following addresses for Alberta's Tax Offices:

Calgary Tax Services Office

Counter/mailing address:
220-4th Avenue South East Calgary AB T2G 0L1
Fax: (403) 264-5843
Hours of service at the counter:
8:15 am to 5:00 pm (mid-February to April 30)
8:15 am to 4:30 pm (May 1 to mid-February)

Edmonton Tax Services Office

Counter/mailing address:
Suite 109, 700 Jasper Avenue Edmonton AB T5J 4C8
Fax: (780) 495-3533
Hours of service at the counter:
8:15 am to 5:00 pm (mid-February to April 30)
8:15 am to 4:30 pm (May 1 to mid-February)

Lethbridge Tax Services Office

Counter address:
200, 419 - 7 Street South Lethbridge AB T1J 4A9
Fax: (403) 382-3052
Mailing address:
PO Box 3009 ST N Main Lethbridge AB T1J 4A9
Hours of service at the counter:
8:15 am to 5:00 pm (mid-February to April 30)
8:15 am to 4:30 pm (May 1 to mid-February)

Red Deer Tax Services Office

Counter/mailing address:
4996-49th Avenue Red Deer AB T4N 6X2
Fax: (403) 341-7053
Hours of service at the counter:
8:15 am to 5:00 pm (mid-February to April 30)
8:15 am to 4:30 pm (May 1 to mid-February)

The following information comes directly from the Canada Revenue Agency Web site: http://www.ccra.gc.ca and is put here to add to your viewing pleasure. Although it is written in government-eze, and may therefore qualify as a sleep aid, Rita strongly recommends reading through it and suggests coffee.

Completing Form RC1, Request for a Business Number (BN)

This is the form (RC1) you'll be filling out in order to register your corporation with the government. This is the form we keep talking about-- the one you get from, and later take to, the place where you register your car. What we're doing here is walking you through the process. Interspersed with the government-eze will be Rita's lovely voice chatting to make things easier.

Since you're becoming a corporation and thus will be communicating with CCRA, you will have to complete Form RC1, Request for a Business Number (BN).

The following information will help you decide which accounts you need and help you complete the form. All businesses have to complete boxes A1 to A5 Part A and sign the certification in Part F. You will have to complete parts B, C, D, or E of the form depending on the type of accounts you need to open.

General information (Part A of the form)

Part A helps identify your business and the nature of its activities.

Box A1 - Identification of business
Enter the legal name and operating or trade name of your business and the business and mailing addresses. We also ask you to identify a contact person.

Business address

The business address is the location of the office where business takes place.

This address will usually be a street address. If the location is a rural route, the address should include the lot and concession number (legal land description). The mailing address is the address where you want them to mail any correspondence. It can be the same as the business address, or it can be a different address.

Contact person

The contact person of a business can be an owner (i.e. a sole proprietor, partner, director, or officer) or an employee who has the information to open an account. (i.e.- **if it's not you, it can be your amazing assistant.***)*

The contact person can register your business, make account enquiries, and update account information without written authorization. You can name contact persons at both the legal entity and program account levels. (i.e.- **your designated person can deal with both your legal stuff and your everyday account stuff or they can deal with one or the other. You get to decide.***)*

The contact person you name at <u>the legal entity level</u> *in Part A of Form RC1* <u>can access all your accounts</u>. <u>Program account contacts</u> *have access* <u>only to their designated accounts</u>. *We provide space in parts B, C, D, and E of the form so that you can name additional contact persons for any of your accounts.*

If you want to authorize a representative who is not an employee of your business to act for you, you have to complete Form RC59, Business Consent Form, or prepare a letter of authorization or equivalent certification and send it to us. An authorized representative, often a lawyer, accountant, customs broker, or tax professional from outside your business, can register your business, access all your BN accounts, make account enquiries, and provide information to update accounts.

Authorized representatives remain authorized until you revoke their authorization.

Another fine tidbit from Rita:
Most of the time, your "authorized representative is you--and only you-- but if you choose to have somebody act on your behalf, that's when this is applicable. If it's you, it's your name on the form. If it's someone else, it's theirs.

Box A2 - Client ownership type
Enter the ownership type of your business, the structure, and the principals. (In plain speak: are you a sole owner of your corporation, or do you have partners? And how is your partnership structured?)

If you have a number of partners, include the names, addresses, and social insurance numbers of corporation directors, partners, or officers as an attachment to the form.

Box A3 - Type of operation
Check the box that best describes your type of operation.

Box A4 - Major commercial activity
Enter your major business activity here and give as much detail as possible. You have to list the products you will sell and estimate the percentage of revenues each product represents. For example, a new art store may estimate revenues of 60% for framed paintings (including original works and prints), 30% for framing services, and 10% for art supplies.

Box A5 - GST/HST information
Everyone has to complete box A5. *If you need a GST/HST account, also complete Part B of the form.*

Note:
There may be circumstances where you have to determine whether you are self-employed or an employee before registering for GST/HST. For example, a real estate agent who earns a commission for sales while working for a known real estate agency may be an employee and not have to register. A quick test would be to determine whether an employer withholds payroll deductions. If you are not sure whether you are an employee or self-employed person, call us at 1-800-959-5525.

Before you complete this section of the form, you need to know basic information about your obligations and entitlements with respect to GST/HST.

For more information, see Chapter 5, GST, on how to fill this in.

Registering for a corporate income tax account (Part E of the form)
If you want to open a corporate income tax account, you should complete Part E of the form. In most cases, new corporations will automatically receive a BN from the CCRA within 45 days of incorporating at the federal or provincial level. All corporations have to provide a copy of the certificate of incorporation or amalgamation. If you need your BN before they send you confirmation that they have opened a corporate income tax account for you, please call the Business Enquiries line at 1-800-959-5525.

What happens after you register?
Soon after you register your corporation and for a BN, they will send you a letter confirming your BN and the accounts you have opened, and a summary of the information you provided on registration.

You can order publications that provide more details about the accounts you open. On your BN application form, just answer "yes" to the question "Do you want us to send you (GST/HST, payroll deductions, or Import/export account) information?)

"Articles of Incorporation"

This form is available online at
http://www3.gov.ab.ca/gs/information/publications/reg_forms.cfm
We also include a copy at the end of this book.\

Step one:
Fill in the corporation name that you searched and were given permission to use at "the place where you register your car".

Step two:
You will enter the type and number of available shares.
Usually there are 100 shares available to be owned by the various partners. Sometimes ownership is decided by how much money each of you puts in to the business, but not always. It can be decided based on sweat equity,

Class A shares –   100 % if you are a sole owner
                                      50% if you have a partner

Class E shares (if you have a partner) – 50%
The above division of shares is an example only, and the shares may be divided differently, as long as they add up to 100 shares. For example: 52/48, 60/40.

Step three:
Restrictions of share Transfers:
No shares can be transferred without the written consent of the majority of the directors.
The number of shareholders may not exceed 15.

Step four:
Number, or minimum and maximum number of directors that the corporation may have:
A minimum of one and a maximum of 10 directors.

Step five:
Certain business or restricted to carrying on a certain business:
None

Step six:
Other rules or provisions:
None

Step seven:
Fill in the blanks for the names of the people involved in incorporating this company, i.e.- the shareholders and all their information including their Social Insurance Number (SIN #) and/or a driver's license #.

and finally:

Step eight:
Sign and date

ALL DONE!!

CHAPTER 5

GST: WHEN, HOW, AND WHERE?

When your company becomes so wonderfully successful that you have made $30,000 in a fiscal year, you are required to collect and pay GST. You have twenty-nine days from the month in which your business has reached that magical $30,000 mark to register with CCRA (Canada Customs and Revenue Agency -- the tax people). You can choose to pay and collect GST prior to the magic number mark (especially if your business is making large item purchases at start up), in order to take advantage of the GST rebate; however, you are not *required* to do so.

How to do this? You must acquire a business number (BN) from the CCRA (the tax people), which we discussed in Chapter 3. You can also decide how often you want to report your GST: yearly or quarterly. Quarterly submissions will break up the sum into more manageable chunks. A yearly submission can be scary. If you're operating more than one division, all income must be combined. Thus, if you're operating Fipke Electrical and Fipke Consulting, and the latter makes $60,000 and the former makes $120,000, then the combined total income is $180,000 and the GST must be calculated and remitted from that amount.

GST Remittance Forms:

The following instructions are not in government-eze. The intent is to explain everything as clearly and as painlessly as possible – it is not hard and if you can work a calculator, you can do this! Here we go…

A sample GST remittance form is shown in the appendix

Line 101 on the GST remittance form,

<u>*Total Sales and Other Revenue*</u> = the total amount of $$ you made during the remitting period. Let's say it is **$180,000.00**

Line 103,

<u>*Total GST amounts collected*</u> during the reporting period (the GST YOU charged your clients for Goods and Services)
Let's say - **$180,000 x 7%= $12,600**

Line 106,

Total GST **you paid** or owe on qualifying expenses (this is any GST your corporation paid out) For the purpose of illustration, let's say your company paid G.S.T. on purchases of goods or services for running your business equaling: **$8000.00**

Line 109,

The difference between 103 and 106 (the amount you now owe)=
$12,600 - $8,000 = $4,600

If done in a yearly installment, you would pay the entire $4,600.00 in one fell swoop. In quarterly installments, the amount becomes much more manageable at $1,150.00 paid at each quarter.

Here is some (unfortunately unavoidable) Government-eze from their website regarding GST. If you have caffeine jitters from the coffee I already recommended, try some tea!!

Most businesses that sell or provide **taxable goods and services** in Canada need a GST/HST account. *Taxable goods and services means goods and services that are taxable at 7%, 15%,* (this 15% is a harmonized provincial tax/GST and is not applicable in Alberta) *and 0% (zero-rated). This **does not** include those that are exempt* (See below for examples of exempt/zero rated items).

Goods and services taxable at 7% or 15%
If you are a GST/HST registrant and you provide goods and services that are taxable at 7% or 15%, you have to charge GST/HST to your clients. You can also claim input tax credits to recover the GST/HST you pay or owe on goods and services you consume, use, or supply in your commercial activities.

Examples of goods and services taxable at 7% or 15% include:
- *commercial rent;*
- *sales and leases of automobiles;*
- *gasoline;*
- *clothing and footwear;*
- *legal and accounting fees;*
- *hotel accommodation; and*
- *advertising.*

Zero-rated goods and services
If you are a GST/HST registrant and you provide zero-rated goods and services, you do not charge GST/HST to your clients but you can claim input tax credits.

Zero-rated goods and services include:
- *basic groceries such as milk, bread, and vegetables;*
- *certain prescription drugs and medical devices;*
- *most farm products and livestock;*
- *most fishery products; and*
- *exports (most goods and services taxable at 7% or 15% in Canada are zero-rated when exported).*

Exempt goods and services

When you provide exempt goods and services, you do not charge GST/HST to your client and you cannot claim input tax credits. In general, when you provide only exempt goods and services, you cannot register for GST/HST.

Examples of exempt goods and services include:
- *long-term residential rents and residential condominium fees;*
- *day-care services provided primarily to children 14 years old and younger;*
- *most medical and dental services;*
- *most financial services; and*
- *legal aid services.*

Do you have to register for GST/HST?

You have to register for GST/HST if you are in one of the following situations:

- *You are an operator of taxi or limousine services (regardless of your revenues).*

- *Your worldwide revenues (and those of your associates) **from taxable goods and services** are more than $30,000 in your last four consecutive calendar quarters or in one single calendar quarter. If you are a public service body (charity, non-profit organization, municipality, public college, university, school authority, or hospital authority), this limit is $50,000. Special rules also apply to charities and public institutions. For more information on how to calculate the $30,000 or $50,000 limit, see the "Small supplier calculation".*

• *You are a non-resident who enters Canada to charge admission directly (the admissions are not made by a resident promoter or ticket agent) to audiences at activities or events in Canada. This rule does not apply if the admissions relate to a convention where at least 75% of the attendees are non-residents of Canada.*

• *You solicit orders in Canada for prescribed goods to be sent to Canada by mail or courier, and your worldwide taxable sales (and those of your associates) are more than $30,000 over the past four consecutive calendar quarters or in a single calendar quarter ($50,000 if you are a public service body). Prescribed goods include printed materials, such as books, newspapers, periodicals, and magazines, and an audio recording that relates to those publications and that accompanies the publications when they are sent to Canada.*

Voluntary registration

Generally, you do not have to register for GST/HST if your worldwide revenues are $30,000 or less ($50,000 for public service bodies). If you do not exceed these limits, you are considered a small supplier. However, you can register voluntarily. You may want to do so for the following reasons:

• *You want to claim input tax credits to recover the GST/HST you pay or owe on your business purchases.*
• *You are starting your business activities and you want to register before your total worldwide revenues of taxable goods and services exceed $30,000 or $50,000.*
• *Your clients may do business only with registered businesses.*

If you decide to register voluntarily, you have to charge, collect, and remit GST/HST on your sales of goods and services that are taxable at 7% or 15%. You will also have to file GST/HST returns on a regular basis.

Note: If you decide to register voluntarily, you have to stay registered for at least one year before you can cancel your registration (unless you stop your commercial activities).

Registering for a GST/HST account (Part B of the form)

This is the form you fill out to actually register for your GST account. It's pretty straightforward. I know you can do it! If you have any problems, you may phone the toll free line @ **1-800-959-5525** where you'll find a "positive plethora of pleasant people" who are all waiting patiently for your call.

If, after completing box A5, you determine that you have to register for GST/HST or you want to register voluntarily, complete Part B of the form.

Box B2 - Filing information
Enter the fiscal year-end date of your business in the first section of box B2. A fiscal year can be either a calendar or non-calendar year. For all businesses, the tax year for income tax purposes is the fiscal year for GST/HST purposes. You can change your GST/HST fiscal year-end by calling 1-800-959-5525 or by filing Form GST70, Election or Revocation of an Election to Change a GST/HST Fiscal Year.

Enter the effective date of registration in the second section of box B2. The effective date of registration for GST/HST is important because it helps set up your reporting requirements, and it establishes the date that you become both liable to collect GST/HST and eligible to claim input tax credits.

If you register on a voluntary basis, you can leave this section blank, and we will enter the date we process your request for a GST/HST account as the effective date. You can, however, choose a later date (e.g., if you have not yet set up your business).

Box B3 - Reporting period

You have to estimate your annual GST/HST annual taxable sales made in Canada in box B3. This amount determines the frequency for filing your GST/HST returns. In this calculation, include your total taxable sales of goods and services made in Canada, including those of your associates. Do not include zero-rated exports, financial services, taxable sales of capital real property, or goodwill. The following chart shows the assigned reporting periods based on the estimation of your revenues and the options available. If you want to change your assigned period, complete the "Options" section in box B3 or call us at 1-800-959-5525.

ASSIGNED REPORTING PERIODS AND OPTIONS

Annual taxable sales	*Assigned Reporting Period*	*Options*
$500,000 or less	*Annual*	*Monthly or Quarterly*
More than $500,000 up to $6,000,000	*Quarterly*	*Monthly*
More than $6,000,000	*Monthly*	*Nil*

We assign an annual reporting period to most financial institutions and to charities regardless of their revenues.

Box B4 - Type of operation

Check the box that best describes your type of operation.

Registering for a payroll deductions account (Part C of the form)

Most employers, trustees, and administrators need a payroll deductions account.

Employers
You are an employer if:
- *you pay a salary, wages (including advances), bonuses, vacation pay, or tips to your employees; or*
- *you provide a benefit, such as board and lodging, to your employees.*

Usually, a person who performs services for you is your employee (engaged under a contract of service). Generally, an employer-employee relationship exists if you have the right to control and direct the person or people who perform the services for you. If you are not sure whether someone is your employee, call the Business Enquiries line at 1-800-959-5525.

Goods and services tax/harmonized sales tax
If you ask for more GST/HST information, we will send you a copy of the guide called General Information for GST/HST Registrants, which explains how GST/HST works. We will also send you an information sheet, GST/HST Options, which discusses the various elections you can make to change your assigned reporting periods, fiscal year, and accounting periods.

CHAPTER 6

TAX MATTERS & YOUR ACCOUNTANT

Corporations **have** to pay tax, but are taxed differently than you, as an individual. All taxpayers, whether individual or corporation, pay federal and provincial taxes; however, the small business tax rate is always lower than personal tax rate. Taxes, as always, are calculated on how much money you make (how much profit). Corporations differ from individuals in that your rate does not increase until you've exceeded $400,000 *in profit*.

These are areas where your accountant will be able to help you and about which he/she *should* be knowledgeable:

➪ Small business deduction – the special lower corporate tax rate on small businesses

➪ Tax deferral strategies – when it's in your best interests, deferring your income-- paying tax later-- so you can accumulate more wealth now and pay less tax.

➪ Income splitting – paying other family members so that all the income is not taxed in your hands

➪ Declaring dividends and bonuses – getting the profits out of the corporation, while paying the least amount of personal and corporate tax.

➪Capital gains – the difference between what was paid for something and what it sold for at the later date – its increase in value.

➪Crystallization of capital gains – avoiding or deferring the payment of tax on capital gains

➪Income smoothing – paying yourself a steady income from year to year, as opposed to having one year with lots of income and another year with only a little bit of income – this would suck!!

➪Expense deductions – income that does not get taxed – it is used to pay your legitimate expenses.

➪Choice of fiscal year-end – paying taxes when it is most convenient for you.

➪Transferring assets into the corporation- selling personally owned assets to the corporation

➪Other less common issues including estate planning, bankruptcy of the corporation, a death of a shareholder; and the sale or death of the corporation.

You can interview an accountant in the same way that you'd interview any employee. If they don't know about these areas, or their knowledge seems weak, move on. Low bidder isn't always your best bet and neither, incidentally, is high bidder. Find out how he/she charges…some accountants charge by "billable hours". This means every time you call them, they will bill you.

Rita says:

With our first Oilfield business, we were new to the accountant world and had a whole lot of questions, so we often called for answers... then the bill arrived. It was HUGE and included billing for every call we had made!! Now I prefer to have an accountant who charges a flat rate for the year that not only includes all my calls, but also the cost of my year-end.

So... *Ask!* Inform yourself. Interview. Create a partnership. This person will become your new best friend and super hero!!

Also, don't think you're economizing by doing it yourself, or that you just can't afford it, or don't need an accountant.

An accountant is crucial and will save you huge amounts of money, headaches, concern, worry, and time. He/she is one of your most valuable assets!!!!

Another tidbit from Rita:

Good accountants know all the current tax laws. Don't forget: it's not only their job to keep abreast of yearly changes, but it's their business to know your business!

And, remember, this book is a general overview of information. **If you have specific questions, or require further information, seek counsel from your well-interviewed lawyer or accountant**....they are an integral part of your success team!

More on taxes

Individuals and corporations MUST pay taxes ..... and the tax people don't have much of a sense of humor. They don't care that business is booming, that you have been way too busy to do your taxes or keep records, that the cat had kittens, or that your Mother-in-law was in town at your year-end and you were so stressed you forgot about it!!

Taxes *must* be filed!! And if you owe $$$, **pay them**. They charge exorbitant interest and even more exorbitant late penalties!! Trust me, it is just easier to do your taxes as quickly as possible after your year-end.

You have to pay Canada Customs and Revenue their portion (Federal Tax), as well as the Province of Alberta's Provincial Tax. Each wants a piece of your $$$ income.

A business is taxed on the **PROFIT** it makes-- not every cent taken in. Its profit is equal to its gross income (or revenue) that the corporation takes in, *minus* its legitimate expenses (the money spent to earn the income). But remember – having to pay taxes is actually a good thing,.. it means you made $$ and are the success we all knew you were going to be!!!!!!

The lower your corporation's profit, the lower your tax bill. How do you lower your profits...*legally*?? There are two ways – the first is not making any $$$$. We don't even want to consider this as an option. With all of our coaching, you are going to be so successful and make so much money that we need another way.

We all want to pay as little tax as possible. We don't want the government to get any more than their fair share of your hard earned money!!

For the record,

Tax avoidance is paying as little tax as is legally required. This is a good thing.

Tax evasion is failing to pay the taxes you are legally required to pay – and this is a <u>BAD</u> thing. You will be talking to us for the next eight to ten from the "**Crow Bar Hilton**" if you do this. Again, your new best friend – your accountant-- will help you to make sure you are legal, and keep you updated on the ever-changing tax laws.

Now, about those *legitimate expenses* – remember you are required by law to support all of your expenses with receipts and appropriate paper work. Fictional accounting will cost you too much in the long run, including your ***integrity***!! It's not worth it.

Another great tip from Rita:

Consider paying your corporate taxes in monthly installments. Somehow, writing a monthly cheque to the government for $1666.67 is a lot easier than a lump sump payment of $20,000.00.

What are legitimate business expenses?

✓ Rent or lease payments on your office/ business space

✓ Cost of labor and materials for maintenance and repairs done to the space you use to earn income

✓ Costs of leased equipment you use in your business

✓ The cost of buying or making the goods you sell

✓ Delivery, shipping, freight costs

✓ Insurance premiums on your building, space, contents, vehicle and equipment

✓Utilities - – water, heat, electricity, telephone, internet, cell phone

✓Office expenses and supplies such as – paper clips, pens, toilet paper and coffee...

✓Some of your vehicle expenses – you use your car to run errands, pick up supplies, go to meetings (client or otherwise), etc.

✓The interest you pay on any loans, or money you borrow to start or run your business.

✓Any annual license fees, municipal taxes, fees or annual dues

✓All your lawyer, accountant, bookkeeping and other professional fees

✓The management and administration expenses to operate your business – including the bank charges, paying the directors to manage the business, etc

✓Advertising expenses

✓Travel expenses incurred to earn business income

✓Fifty percent of business meals, beverages and entertainment.

✓Salaries and benefits paid to your hard working and loyal employees, and your portion of their Canada Pension Plan and Employment Insurance premiums...see **Employees section**.

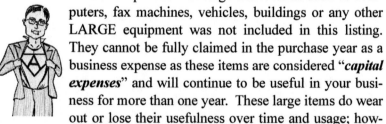

You will notice that the purchase of large ticket items such as computers, fax machines, vehicles, buildings or any other LARGE equipment was not included in this listing. They cannot be fully claimed in the purchase year as a business expense as these items are considered "*capital expenses*" and will continue to be useful in your business for more than one year. These large items do wear out or lose their usefulness over time and usage; however, so you may claim a percentage of the initial cost as a business expense each year for several years until the entire cost has been claimed. The amount you are allowed to claim on *depreciable capital property* is called *capital cost allowance* and there is a special place on your tax form for calculating the exact amount that you can claim in a given year. We suggest you don't worry your pretty little head over this too much as your new best friend and super hero, **Accountant-Man**, will deal with this!! It is important that you have some idea of what he/she is talking about and what this is when you see it on your tax return.

Some of the items or services you claim as a business expense are also used by you personally - such as your vehicle or cell phone- so you are only allowed to claim the portion of the expense that relates to your business use. If you use your cell phone to make any personal calls, you must deduct that time or percentage of usage from the total cost of your monthly airtime. The rest is business expense.

A New Tidbit From Rita:

When my cell phone bill comes, I highlight any personal calls, and then deduct the cost of them from the total bill. If all my calls are within the limits of my cell phone plan, then I decide the percentage used personally and deduct that amount from the total. I then write a personal cheque to pay the personal part of the bill and a company cheque to pay the business part. Amazingly enough, when I look at my phone bill, almost all of my calls are related to business in one-way or another. Hmmmm-- guess I'm a work-a-holic!!

http://www.cra-arc.gc.ca/E/pub/tg/t4002/t4002-04e.pdf
This is a great site to read all the government –eze about legitimate business expenses and deductions. It is a .pdf file (meaning, you need Adobe, which is a free download) and is pretty easy to follow and read.

This is the Canada Customs and Revenue formal take on business expenses and is worth reading through... *once*. It explains all the legal business deductions in "government-eze" but it will save you a lot of headaches if you are familiar with their wording and the limits that are placed on expenses.

We recommend that you have a nap first – so you are fresh and your brain is working. Additional coffee is recommended, but not requisite.

Home office

Please note: You can use the home office deduction to reduce your taxes to zero, but not to put your business into a loss situation *and* once your profit is reduced to zero, any home office expenses that are left over can be applied against business income in future years.

Vehicle expenses

You are allowed to deduct the expenses of running your vehicle-- as either a per kilometer charge or by keeping track of actual receipts – if you use it to earn business income.

You can (legitimately) claim:
✓ Fuel
✓ Oil changes, oil
✓ Insurance
✓ Repairs and maintenance (tires, etc)
✓ License and registration fees
✓ Leasing costs or interest on the loan for your amazing car
✓ The capital cost allowance, if you purchased your car.

Most often you will be using the vehicle you currently own and will log all the *business usage kilometers*. You will then charge the company for these kilometers. You still pay for the gas, oil changes, tires, insurance, etc.

Often the company will decide that it will have a vehicle of its own -- then the company buys the gas, the oil changes, the insurance, etc and you will have to log any personal usage kilometers that this vehicle makes and you personally will be responsible for paying this to the company. Sometimes people will decide to have all their vehicles owned by the company...***not a good idea***.

You then have to be supremely careful about your personal miles and Revenue Canada frowns on the practice a whole bunch....

Eating Crow! Yeesh!

Rita has some friends who had all their vehicles owned by their company. They were audited because of this and had to pay back an exorbitant amount of estimated personal use mileage. Because the auditor already had his nose in their business, he took a look around at the rest of their life and made it very difficult over a boat they owned. The auditor warned them that they could not use the company truck to tow the boat without being in violation. The family ended up with the choice of purchasing a personal vehicle capable of towing said boat or selling the boat altogether... neither one being a choice they would have made without "persuasion".

So... before you make any big changes regarding the ownership of your vehicles, check with your accountant Super Hero "Accountant Man" as these tax laws change frequently. You want to make sure your information is current for your situation.

If you use your car for both business and personal use, only the portion that you use the vehicle for business is deductible. Just keep all of your receipts and keep track of your business related mileage. This allows you to figure the percentage of business use of your personal vehicle and therefore how much of your total vehicle expenses are legitimate business deductions.

Janet says:

Learn from my mistakes... if you're operating as a sole proprietor or as a partnership, keep your vehicle receipts!! Once upon a time, any business could log mileage and charge per kilometer. No longer! Now, only corporations can choose this option (for business use of personally owned vehicles). I found out the hard way!

Another fantastic tidbit from Rita:

I log the personal use miles on my van because, for me, it's easier. At tax time, I simply subtract those miles from the total miles accumulated, leaving the business miles as a remainder. It seems that most of my usage is business. Again, I guess I am a work- a-holic!!? ☺

For the math majors in the group, take the total car expenses and multiply them by the kilometers driven for business purposes (ie- total kilometers driven minus personal usage). Take this product and *divide it by the total kilometers driven. This leaves you with your allowable vehicle business expense.* For the rest of us, Accountant Man will come to the rescue.

Employee salaries

All expenses related to having an employee are deductible, including the employer's portion of Canada Pension Plan and Employment Insurance premiums. If you are a generous employer and give them benefits – these too are deductible.

A good way to reduce your business income is to hire one of your family members. Pay your spouse (or child) to do tasks around the office, such as filing, errands, mail-outs, putting on stamps, etc …and you will reduce your taxable income. Your family member **will** have to pay personal tax on this income, but, if you keep their income within the lowest tax bracket, their taxes will be nominal. Once again check this out with your best friend and super hero – Accountant Man. The laws on this change frequently. Remember, the family member has to actually receive the income, they actually have to do something for it, and the salary has to be reasonable in comparison to what you would pay someone else.

How much tax will you pay??

If your business has made a profit, it has to pay tax on the profits….a time for celebration!! Your business is a success. We knew it would be.

Corporations are taxed at a flat rate, which can change yearly; however, the small business deduction (discussed earlier) reduces the tax rate to something very manageable.

If your company is not doing so well and you have a loss – a common occurrence in the first year or so of doing business because of all those start up expenses-- the loss can be carried forward and applied against profits made in the next seven years. Conversely, if you've been in business for a while and have a bad year, the loss can be carried back and applied against profits made in the past three years. (Super hero can help you decide.)

Remember that you, as a director of the corporation, have to pay tax on income you have received from the company. Any salary, benefits, bonuses or dividends have to be reported on a T4 or T4A and taxed at your personal tax rate. Once again, if you keep this income below the current lowest tax bracket your tax bill will be minimal.

If you pay yourself dividends, there is a dividend tax credit that limits your tax payable. The tax credit recognizes that these dividends are a "distribution of your corporation's profits", on which the corporation has already paid taxes. In simple terms, this is your share of the company's profits and said company has already paid the lion's share of taxes on this money, so your tax responsibility is minimal.

When and how do you have to pay taxes

Every person is required by Canadian law to file taxes from the previous year on or by April 30th. Every corporation is required to file a tax return from the previous fiscal year within six months of its corporate year-end. Should you owe the CCRA money, you must pay it within three months of your year-end. If you can't get your books done by then, you must estimate the tax owing and submit that amount. Then, when you *do* get the returns done, you must pay the amount left owing, plus interest from the time of your year-end. If you *over* estimated – you will get a refund from CCRA for the difference, but *they* don't have to pay you interest.

Personally, I recommend that you get the returns done within the three months. Sometimes this means you have to put pressure on your new best friend- Accountant Man – but do it anyway. It will save you muchly in interest fees and worry. I also recommend that after your first year, you make the monthly installments CCRA recommends. Paying a little each month is a whole lot easier to handle in most cases, than a big tax bill at year-end.

Another benefit of the monthly installment plan (assuming you've paid enough), is that the government considers your taxes already paid, leaving you with the six months we talked about earlier to get your returns filed... leaving your super-hero best friend in a better mood.

Your year-end is stressful enough with all the insurances coming due, paying your new best friend for all his/her hard work all year and all the other year-end expenses. Spreading things out by paying your taxes in installments helps to relieve the pressure. Should you have a record breaking year, however, the company will be required to pay more tax than estimated and then the three month rule comes into effect again.

How to get into trouble with CCRA

✓ Don't pay your taxes. Period.
✓ Don't make your installment payments on time. (This is also a great way to get flagged for an audit.)
✓ Don't pay enough in installments
✓ Don't pay the balance of tax owing by the due date of three months after your fiscal year-end. You will be charged interest of 10% on any overdue taxes.

You may be charged penalties if:

✓Your accumulated interest charges are over $1000.00 for any year.

✓You file a late return. (Also a good way to get audited)

✓You fail to report income received.

✓You knowingly or carelessly make false statements or omissions on your tax return. (ie- you lie, or pretend you didn't know)

Penalties start at 5% of unpaid taxes, and the fines go up from there, depending upon how BAD you were.

Rita's Tips On Avoiding The Auditor:

Always, always, always file on time. A late Income Tax Return always gets special attention, which you don't want, and the attention can cost you outrageously. If you owe any money, do everything you can to pay it with the return. If you just can't pay, send in the return on time anyway with a letter informing them how you are going to look after the taxes due. Never, never avoid filing because you don't have the money at present.

Another great site to check out for a huge amount of business information and links to reports, tax strategy info, etc. is:

http://sbinfocanada.about.com/

This is an awesome site with an incredible amount of usable information. Rita says: _everyone_ needs to check it out!

Keeping Books

Since you are required to pay taxes and GST, it will be a whole lot easier if you keep a set of books, tracking income and expenses. The system can be as simple or as complicated as you decide. It can be a simple ledger (the old fashioned pencil, ledger and calculator method), a simple excel spread sheet (the modern version of a ledger), or any of the accounting programs out there on the market. You may want to discuss this with your new best friend to see what she uses –it is very convenient to be compatible with your best friend's system.

Keep your invoices and receipts in a file/shoebox – just in case they are needed to support the returns at a later date. All of this (paper and computor disks) must be kept for at least six years after the taxation year they relate to.

What if your worst nightmare comes true and you are audited?
Panic!

Okaaay.... STOP! Now, breathe and read:
When you file your corporation's income tax return, it is reviewed by the CCRA and a notice of assessment is issued. This sets out the amount of tax you need to pay each month for the next year. The CCRA is all-powerful and has the right to reassess your return at a later date and up to three years previous—*longer, if they suspect you have been fraudulent.*

If you get audited, this is a different story. The CCRA will send you a letter identifying the year being audited and you will have 30 days to get all your books in order. **Call your accountant immediately!!** You will then meet with the auditor – not always a pleasant experience (can you say *understatement*?) as he/she is used to dealing with people who lie, cheat and steal so he/she believes you are one of them. He/she will go over all your books and records with a fine-tooth comb and magnifying glass-- everything you have in your shoeboxes, filing cabinets etc...down to the penny -- to see whether you have declared all of your income and deducted **only** legitimate expenses. If you are honest and up front, you will have nothing to hide!! By keeping good records of income and expenses, you can easily prove your honesty. Being able to answer their questions will make the whole experience much more pleasant for all of you.

Another Tidbit From Rita:

Keeping good records is important. Write on the back of receipts or invoices if it's for anything out of the ordinary. This will help you remember what it was about in case of an audit.

If you pretend that you are being audited this year, what information would you need to be able to answer all the questions an auditor might ask about your business and its receipts and invoices?

Remember: the auditor is a detective who can be rather unscrupulous in asking anything and everything *about* anything and everything. Why open the door to this awful experience? Keep things legal, fair and above-board.

Setting up your bookkeeping system

Your bookkeeping system totally depends on you and your business. As we talked about in tax matters, there are as many different methods as there are companies. Once again, check with your new best friend to see what he/she recommends for you. Being compatible with Accountant Man is the wise thing to do.

Before anything else, you must save all the little pieces of paper and put them in a box, a file, a drawer or anywhere that you can access easily at month end. Decide who is going to be your resident book-keeper or hire an outside service.

A Tip From Rita
(and the Chicken, cuz we like the
"wise chick"):

When my bank statements come each month, it reminds me to reconcile my bankbook and do the books. The bank statement has so much of your information on it that having it in hand can make the books easier to do.

Also, if you are hiring someone outside your business to do the books, take the time to sort your receipts, invoices, etcetera into categories and write their purpose on the back of them. This will save you being charged for the time it would take the accountant/book-keeper to figure things out.

Opening your first bank account

Now that you are a corporation and are an amazing success, you need a place to deposit all the income you will be making and a place to write cheques from to pay your bills. This means you will have to open a bank account. I recommend shopping around and see who will give you the best program for your specific situation as every institution has a different method of charging fees and paying interest as well as other services. Make sure you are getting what you want.

And don't be afraid to let them know how successful your idea is going to be and that you are shopping for the best service. They will want your business, and will compete to get it.

To open the account, the bank will need a copy of your "articles of incorporation" – the paper that says that you are a legal corporation, and that you are a legal shareholder/director of the company. (You will have received this from the government when you filed the paper work to set up your incorporation).

When you make/have a sale, the money should be deposited right away into the business bank account, using your business deposit slip book, and then the deposit amount written on the current cheque stub.

Make as many payments by cheque as is possible – it is the best way to track your expenses and expenditures.

Rita says:

Sometimes I run into these really amazing people who can keep track of all of their financial information via the internet and ATM slips. I find it much too complicated; however, as it carries way too much risk of missing something (losing an ATM slip or forgetting what a transaction was for) when entering the data into the bookkeeping system. Also, I've found that when I pay bills online, I don't always keep a record of the transactions.

Your monthly bank statements, deposit book and cancelled cheques are the simplest ways to track what and where you spent your hard earned dollars.

If you use a credit card for paying for your purchases – i.e. fuel, hotels and buying that new client dinner-- it is best to have a separate card for your business. Keep all the receipts so you can reconcile them to the credit card statement at month end.

Another Tip from Rita:

Taking the time to reconcile my credit card statements with the receipts has saved my bacon at least once. I clip the receipts directly onto the statement, making it easy to identify any charges that are not mine. It also makes it easy to identify what the purchases were for and where to allocate them in my book keeping system.

If you use a credit card for both personal and business use, highlight all the business use and then pay that portion with a business cheque and the personal portion with a personal cheque.

If you inadvertently happen to lose one of the receipts, at least, write on the statement what the expenditure was for. It is always a good idea to write on the back of any receipt what you did and with whom in case of nasty auditors.

If you pay for company purchases with personal cash, keep the receipt, write "paid with personal cash" across it and then write your-self a company cheque to repay yourself.

Sorting your income and expenses by category

You will need to sort all those expenses and income into accounting categories in order to be able to prepare taxes, financial statements and to track how your business is doing.

Income
What is considered business income?
Obviously any money made from sales of product or fees for services that you are in the business of selling.

All the money your business takes in will not be identical. Some will be from sales of your product or service. Some will be GST you charged and GST rebates. Some will be returns of products, money you have invested in the business, etc. This all needs to be entered into your bookkeeping system, so sort all the income by the afore-mentioned types of categories.

Expenses
You also will have a number of different types of expenses incurred to operate your business. Some of these will be :

• General expenses:
  Rent
  Office supplies
  Legal and accounting fees
  Advertising and promotions
  Wages paid to employees
  Interest on borrowed money
  Manufacturing costs
  Inventory costs
  Auto expenses

- Home office expenses – the portion of household expenses that can be deducted
- Business entertainment - only 50 percent of this is deductible from income – so keep this one very separate
- Capital expenses – purchase of large, long term use equipment
- GST and tax installment payments
- Health Care Premiums

If you separate all your receipts into these types of files, it will help you, the bookkeeper and your accountant to verify expenses.

All of this information will be entered into your accounting system – be it a ledger or accounting software program. Initially, it may seem overwhelming-- and it can be--but doesn't have to be. Keep it as simple as you can and talk with your best friend, the accountant. She will help you a whole bunch. If book-keeping is beyond your scope of expertise or desire, hire someone competent to do it for you. It should not cost more than $100/month for a basic data entry service. If you require them to pay your bills and do deposits, and everything else that needs to be done, then be prepared to pay more. If you are just too busy doing your business – this can be a lifesaver!!

CHAPTER 7

RUNNING YOUR BUSINESS AS A BUSINESS

Home based office:

If you're running your business out of your home, it's a good idea to have a dedicated space in which to work-- not your dining room table. There is a home business tax deduction, which allows you to deduct a percentage of your home expenses (power, gas, property taxes, electricity, repairs and maintenance, home insurance, mortgage or rent). To calculate the deduction, take the sum of all expenses and divide by the percentage of your home's space that is occupied by the office. Another *"good" thing.*

Phone line:

If you're operating out of your house, you do not want to be paying the phone company for a separate line unless you make and receive a ton of phone calls. You do, however, want to differentiate between personal calls for your teenagers and business calls.

The simplest way to do this is to get a *Smart Ring* feature installed on your home phone by your telephone service provider (e.g..- Telus). This allows you to have a second phone number with a distinctive double ring to notify you when a customer/client is calling. It's also considerably cheaper than a second phone line or, **shudder**, a business line.

An alternate to this is setting up your <u>cell</u> <u>phone</u> as your business phone, especially if you're out of the office a lot. A good Plan here can save you a lot of money. Every three or four months, call your provider and optimize your plan. This can save you huge $$.

Remembering to have voice mail/"electronic secretary" to receive messages when you are out of the office is "a good thing" because you don't want to miss that most important client when they call. Caller ID is also helpful in identifying the type of caller. For example, whether it's a telemarketer, the local newspaper calling to try and sell you this week's advertising special, or, if it's a potential client. You need to know the difference, so that not only do you answer the phone accordingly (using your best business voice), but you can also choose whether or not to interrupt the work you're currently involved in to answer the phone.

Computer:

Your computer is now a corporate item, if you use it to send / receive e-mails to / from clients, print invoices, keep track of expenses and income, etc, etc which of course you do! As you, personally, are selling your computer to your corporation, the corporation owes you money for the computer. You get to decide what the computer's current value is and it goes on your company books as a shareholder's loan to be paid back when the company has money. The corporation will require an invoice for its records, which you can produce on said computer. Don't forget the printer, scanner, fax machine, surge pro-tector, internet hook up/phone line/service fees, desk the computer sits on, the chair the operator sits on, the lamp the operator sees by and perhaps the coffee cup he/she drinks out of. If you're a portable office, your laptop, cell phone, palm pilot, any wireless paraphernalia, and any related software is fair game.

If you use your fax a lot, which is doubtful in this day of email, have a dedicated fax line. It is more professional than the alternative of having to ask your client to phone first, so you can plug in your fax machine. Computer faxing is most convenient and saves paper and ink. Bite the bullet and learn how to run it.

Running your business as a business:

Remembering to be professional is always a challenge when you're running your business out of your home and by yourself. Even simple things, like being aware of the type of music/noise that is playing in the background, when answering your phone is important. Setting business hours helps to keep you organized and on track. There's a risk of either procrastinating, and not working your business or, conversely, working all the time. Setting an office structure helps to encourage you to do this.

Don't forget to take coffee breaks. You'll work better. You won't feel so overwhelmed or exhausted. Go for lunch occasionally. Get out of the office. See people. Go for a walk.

Make sure you keep in touch with colleagues. Network. Maintain professional connections. It keeps you motivated, inspired and helps prevent burnout. Networking is also hugely important in the expansion of your client base and any money you spend on affiliations/memberships will come back to you tenfold. These events are not a cost to you or your business in regards to time and money. They are an investment in you – your most precious asset and the future of your business.

Insurance:

You may wonder why you will need insurance, but bad things do happen to good people and we have to guard against fire, theft, mudslides, volcanoes, hurricanes, tornadoes and other unforeseen events. No one wants to think about, or plan for, a death or sudden illness of partner, but failing to plan for the financial and legal issues can be a huge headache that you don't want. Don't go there. Protect yourself.

- If your business involves giving advice then you should have insurance against giving bad advice.
- If you manufacture a product – you should have insurance against defective parts.
- If you have clients or customers coming into your premises – you should have insurance against injuries that could occur there.
- As well you'll need the usual theft, fire, flood, etc

Review your insurance each year, as your needs might change as your business grows.

If you are doing business out of your home –speak with your current household insurance provider –often they can do an add-on to your current policy that won't cost an arm and a leg. The most important thing here is to talk with your insurance provider, and again don't be afraid to shop around…don't take the first option, often there are more choices than you had realized and of course related variations in costs.

Your *household insurance* does not cover all of your office stuff if you don't have a conversation with your insurance agent. Just by letting them know you have a home-based business allows them to include it on your policy and quite often there's no cost increase (depending upon your situation), but they have to know. If you have customers and clients, this will also impact the type of insurance that you need.

Things you need to insure:

Office contents including computers, fax machine, office equipment (basically, all of the things you wrote off as business expenses).

Also, if you're driving your car for business purposes, there are insurance implications, so be sure to let your insurance provider know. This will cost you money, but if you have an accident, and they can prove you were on your way to do business, you're in a mess and they may not honour your insurance coverage.

You'll also need *liability insurance*, if you have clients coming to your home (in case someone slips on the ice). It can also protect your family against personal liability. *Disability insurance* replaces your business income should you be disabled (this is optional, but can be important to look at), *critical illness insurance* is a newer option, but it is popular as it protects should you be diagnosed with cancer, heart attack or stroke or whatever.

You may also want to purchase a *shareholder's life insurance* policy that includes a buy-sell agreement in case one of your shareholders becomes incompetent, dies, or something else unforeseen but terrible happens so that you can keep the business operating. A buy-sell agreement allows the surviving partner(s)/shareholders to legally purchase the shares of the deceased at a fair market price. This will help deal with any tax implications and offset the tax liability.

Talk to your insurance provider about these options. It may save you a lot of head/heart aches. Don't leave yourself vulnerable. And once again, feel free to shop around!!

Other things

Business license:

You need to get a business license from your local city/town/ municipality, which lets them know that you're doing business, even if it's out of your home. Often this requires a letter sent out to your neighbours, which in effect asks their permission for you to conduct business out of your home. If they object, they can send a letter to the town office/city hall, saying why they object and your business license can be rejected based on that objection (and its validity). Should City Hall decide that the objection is frivolous, they may ignore it and grant your license anyway.

Year End:

It is not necessary, nor desirable to have your year end on December 31st. Consider a time when your accountant will be less busy -- April is **not** a good time. Having a year-end after July 31st and before December 31st allows your accountant time enough to plan your taxes and/or tax strategies to your highest benefit. By planning your year-end in a slower season, it allows more time to meet with your accountant, catch up on inventory and do the all and sundry year-end tasks.

CHAPTER 8

PAYING YOURSELF: GETTING $$ OUT OF YOUR CORPORATION

Now that you are a registered, legally operating corporation, you are doing great business by selling your product or service out there in the market place. You are making money and you want to take some home to feed the dog, the kids, pay the mortgage, etc....*imagine that!!* Keeping in mind, of course, that you cannot just "take it"— that it is the corporation's money, not yours--here are the four most commonly used ways of paying yourself:

Payment of salary - you are paid for being an officer or employee. This salary is fully tax deductible to the corporation and is fully taxable in your hands as income received as salary and T4s will have to be issued by the corporation regarding the salary. (Eww! This involves lots of book keeping, filing and paying of monthly deductions (CPP, EI) *and* necessitates a high personal tax bracket! Eww, again!)

Bonuses can also be paid to officers or employees. These are taxed the same as paid salary and added to taxable income. The tax department frowns on paying spouses (or others who do not have much to do with the business, including the dog) huge bonuses. Keep the bonuses to your active participants. A watchdog could be included, but it's a definite gray area!

Dividends (Rita's Favourite) are payments to the shareholders out of the profits of the corporation where the corporation pays the tax on these profits first at the lower corporate tax rate. As this dividend amount is not a tax-deductible expense for the corporation, it first pays the tax at its nice low rate of small business taxation and *then* pays the dividends out to the shareholders.

The dividend is then taxed (in your hands) at a special low rate for the shareholders' personal taxes. Your accountant will be able to help you decide exactly how to do this.

Another something to crow about:

When you take money out of your corporation as "dividends", you don't have to pay EI (which you can't claim anyway when you're self-employed) or CPP if you don't believe it's going to be there for you when you retire-- another saving!

There can be great tax advantages to paying yourself, as a shareholder, in this manner.

Let's say Barry is a contractor whose company has a profit of $20,000/month. That $20,000 immediately goes into the corporation's bank account, which then pays for Barry's company truck, tools, fuel, taking the current client out to lunch or what have you. Barry and his lovely wife each take home (as equal shareholder's in the corporation) $2000/month in dividends. The company has paid tax (at its wonderful low rate) before Barry or his lovely wife have even seen their dividend cheques and at year-end, the happy couple will each pay a minimal amount of personal tax, because anything claimed as dividends has already had the majority of the required tax paid on it.

If there is anything else you do in your life to make money, those funds will add to the amount of personal tax you're due to pay. Situations do vary, however, depending upon how you've set up your corporate structure and current tax laws. Remember: your accountant is your best friend and can make your fiscal heart flutter. Be nice to him/her!

Shareholders' loans

These are the amounts owed to you, the shareholders, by the corporation--usually money and/or assets you put into the company at start-up. The corporation can decide to pay this back to you at any time there is enough funds in the coffers to do so. The corporation will pay tax on the money it repays to you, but you do not have to pay tax on it when you take it back, because you paid tax on it when you got it initially. Again, discussion with Accountant Man, your new best friend, will help you decide when it is best to do this.

CHAPTER 9

EMPLOYEES AND PAYROLL

If, on the outside chance, you have employee/s, you must withhold and submit payroll deductions like C.P.P., E.I. and taxes. This can seem daunting. Sometimes it is. Getting an accountant/bookkeeper or a really good payroll computer program helps make the headache go away. The government is always changing the structure and rates of its deductions, wanting to get the biggest piece of your dollar that it can. You will want to be up to date on current regulations as your employees will be responsible for your screw ups and no one's going to be very happy about a large unexpected tax bill if you don't deduct enough each month.

When you registered your company, you received your business number and you automatically started receiving information about payroll from the government. If you have employees, pay attention to the stuff you get. We recommend opening it and reading it. Your accountant, again, is your best friend and can help you set up your structure for this.

You may find it easier, and more advantageous, to "contract" out the services you require. Your contractors are then responsible for keeping track of their own stuff, and, you're actually helping them out because now they can be a company and enjoy the inherent tax benefits therein.

Talk to your "super hero" about this and whether it can be applied to you and your situation as there are rules around this that often change. He/she can be a great help here.

Payroll deductions

If you ask for more payroll information, we will send you a copy of the employers' guides called Payroll Deductions (Basic Information) and Remitting Payroll Deductions, which contain details about the income tax, Canada Pension Plan contributions, Quebec Pension Plan contributions, and Employment Insurance premiums that employers, trustees, and administrators have to deduct and remit.

You will also receive the payroll deductions tables to help you calculate your employees' deductions. You can get these tables in two formats: paper or Windows diskette.

Unless you are a large employer, we have to receive deductions on or before the 15th day of the month after the month that the employer, trustee, or administrator paid the remuneration. If the due date falls on a Saturday, Sunday, or holiday, the remittance is due on the next working day. The exception to this rule is for large employers, who have to remit more often. The rules for all employers are explained in the employers' guide called Payroll Deductions (Basic Information). www.ccra.arc.gc.ca

Note: If you open a payroll deductions account and are then delayed in hiring your employees, you should notify us. Otherwise, you will receive a notice asking for your first payment.

If you happen to open a Payroll deductions account and then you and your partner become the only people working for the company, just send them a letter stating that you no longer have employees and you will let them know when and if you will have employees in the future. Calling them works, too. 1-800-959-5525.

Business Plan:

Now that your business is all set up, we need to be sure that you are the amazing success we know you can be, so the next step should be the creation of your business plan.

*A Business Plan? What the @#** is that?*

Isn't writing a business plan hard and boring??? Not so, Grasshopper. You can even make it "somewhat" exciting. Just think: it is the planning, creating and envisioning of your business, its future and its success!!

A business plan is a written document outlining your ideas for the future and how you plan on getting there. It can be a single page document or a small book-- depending upon how detailed and complete you decide to be with it. I recommend doing a deep and comprehensive one at the start-up of your business. This helps you clarify how you expect and/or want your business to run.

While preparing your business plan, try to put yourself in the shoes of the reader. Ask yourself, "As an investor, would I finance this business based on the information provided?"

Remember that potential lenders and investors don't know your business as well as you do, so try to give as much information (based on fact and research) as possible. Pretending you are going to borrow money, even if you never have to, is a great way to do a business plan.

Finally, as your business grows and your environment and objectives change, it is important to update your business plan to reflect those changes.

There are many places to get a Business plan outline or form:
• You can find booklets to complete from your local bank.
• You can purchase Business Plan computor programs.
• You can go online to various places to find them.

A few online choices for free, downloadable business plan program/forms are:
• Alberta Women Entrepreneurs
  http://www.awebusiness.com/
•The Royal Bank has a great one…it is easy to follow
  http://www.rbcroyalbank.com/sme/
•From the TD Bank –
  http://www.tdcanadatrust.com/smallbusiness/windocs.jsp

The most important thing… is to sit down and write the plan. It *will* be time consuming and sometimes frustrating, but you will learn a lot about yourself, your business and where and/or how it is going to be successful. (Better to find this out now, before you've lost money to poor planning!) I recommend having a friend or associate help out with this process. It makes it much more fun and the questions they ask can often help clarify your plan, catch any missed details and help flesh out your ideas and goals. Put on a big pot of coffee or tea, sharpen your pencil and… ***go for it!***

ABOUT THE AUTHORS...

Rita Fipke is a seasoned businesswoman who has created—and helped others create-- numerous corporations. She is a heartfelt, authentic speaker and author and is the founder of a successful Alberta-wide coaching practice. Based out of Calgary, she coaches clients from all walks of life on personal and business related matters. Rita offers the world her warm and enthusiastic approach to growth and learning in a fun, interactive environment.

Together, Rita and her husband, Ron, have succeeded in (and thoroughly enjoyed!) their thirty-year adventure in marriage, child rearing and making a living in the oil patch. During that time, they successfully started, operated, and eventually sold three oilfield service companies. She currently manages both Ron's consulting business and her own practice. As well, having built a successful network marketing business, Rita believes that being with a good company of that type is a great place to acquire valuable business skills.

Rita's background includes a huge number of business development courses, including:

- Oracle Education's — *Fundamental Real Estate Training*
- Bob Proctor's — *You Were Born Rich*
  — *The Liberty League*
- Robert Kiyosaki — *The Advanced Skills of Technical Investing*
- Mark Victor Hansen — *Mastermind Your Way to Millions*
- Peak Potentials': — *Train the Trainer*
  — *Wealth and Wisdom*
  — *Millionaire School*
  — *Wealth creation: investment courses and trainings*

- regular investment trainings and information sessions, sponsored by the *Freedom Investment Club* to keep abreast of changes and opportunities as they occur.

In addition to her coaching practice and adventures in book writing, Rita currently facilitates a number of workshops, retreats, and seminars – from small, intimate ones to larger, corporate ones -to help build skills and success for individuals, teams, and organizations.

For more information, you can learn more about Rita at
www.transformationsnaturally.ws

Janet MacLeod has been a researcher, a teacher, a home-schooling mom, a librarian, an historian and a used car salesperson (amongst a myriad of other things), but she always comes back to writing. For her, it's a place of joy.

Janet started her love affair with words many, many years ago--in grade three- with the following sentence:
> When dinosaurs roamed the earth,
> man lived in fear.

It was the first line of a report on Tyrannosaurus Rex and even if she did fail the assignment due to a lamentable lack of imagination in educators of that era (and a teeny, tiny problem with historical accuracy), she still thinks it's a kick butt opening-- especially for an eight year old. (She has since become much more diligent in checking her facts.)

Janet came to the project with a number of years of research and writing experience. She wrote a popular weekly newspaper column for three years, took time to learn the Ukrainian and Russian languages in Kiev and-- after earning her degree-- taught English, Second Languages, Social Studies and Creative Writing to grade two through grade twelve and adult upgrading. She has completed a number of research and writing contracts for the provincial government and the University of Alberta's Folklore Department, and opened the doors of Audio Legacy, a family history recording venture, in October of 2004. She is immensely proud of her one-of-a-kind business and its ability to capture (and preserve) the spirit, the stories and the voice of families across Alberta. You can find more information about her company and why this form of history is so important to her at: www.audiolegacy.ca.

She is married, with one daughter.

WORTH INVESTIGATING....

Voth, David. M., <u>The 10 Secrets Revenue Canada Doesn't Want YOU To Know</u>.
     e-mail - libertyhouse@shaw.ca

Kerr, Margaret and Jo Ann Kurtz, <u>Canadian Small Business Kit for Dummies</u>.
     www.kerr-and-kurtz.com

The Legal Ease Library Inc., <u>Incorporating and Organizing a Corporation</u>,

This is a good resource of all the forms, etc that you will need. You can get the kit at the place where you register your car....

Ecker, T. Harv, <u>Secrets of the Millionaire Mind, Mastering the Inner Game of Wealth</u>
     www.peakpotentials.com

Loral Langemeier (speaker, author, business coach, real person)
Loral has a wide array of proven business strategies, tactics and ideas to help make your dreams a reality.
     http://www.liveoutloud.com

BIBLIOGRAPHY

Kerr, Margaret and JoAnn Kurtz, <u>Canadian Small Business Kit for Dummies</u>, Copyright: CDG Books Canada, Inc., 2002.
www.kerr-and-kurtz.com ISBN 1-894413-04-0

The Legal Ease Library Inc., <u>Incorporating and Organizing a Corporation</u>, Copyright: The Legal Ease Library Inc, Calgary, Alberta, 2002.

Canada Customs and Revenue Agency: www.ccra.gc.ca

APPENDICES:

Keep Your Sanity and Your Shirt

Industry Canada Industrie Canada	FORM 1	FORMULAIRE 1
Canada Business Loi canadienne sur les Corporations Act sociétés par actions	ARTICLES OF INCORPORATION (SECTION 6)	STATUTS CONSTITUTIFS (ARTICLE 6)

1 -- Name of the Corporation | Dénomination sociale de la société

2 -- The province or territory in Canada where the registered office is situated | La province ou le territoire au Canada où est situé le siège social

3 -- The classes and any maximum number of shares that the corporation is authorized to issue | Catégories et le nombre maximal d'actions que la société est autorisée à émettre

4 -- Restrictions, if any, on share transfers | Restrictions sur le transfert des actions, s'il y a lieu

5 -- Number (or minimum and maximum number) of directors | Nombre (ou nombre minimal et maximal) d'administrateurs

6 -- Restrictions, if any, on the business the corporation may carry on | Limites imposées à l'activité commerciale de la société, s'il y a lieu

7 -- Other provisions, if any | Autres dispositions, s'il y a lieu

8 -- Incorporators - Fondateurs

Name(s) - Nom(s)	Address (including postal code) Adresse (inclure le code postal)	Signature	Tel. No. - N° de tél.

FOR DEPARTMENTAL USE ONLY - À L'USAGE DU MINISTÈRE SEULEMENT

IC 3419 (2004/12)

Canada

Articles of Incorporation
1

Canada Business Corporations Act	Loi canadienne sur les sociétés par actions
Articles of Incorporation **FORM 1** **INSTRUCTIONS**	**Statuts constitutifs** **FORMULAIRE 1** **INSTRUCTIONS**

General
If you require more information in order to complete Form 1, you may wish to consult the Incorporation Kit and the Name Granting Compendium or the Name Granting Guidelines.

You can file Form 1 through the Corporations Canada On-line Filing Centre at http://strategis.ic.gc.ca/corporations or you can send or fax the completed documents to the address provided below.

Prescribed Fees
Corporations Canada On-line Filing Centre: $200
By mail or fax: $250

Item 1
Set out the proposed corporate name that complies with sections 10 and 12 of the Act. Articles of incorporation must be accompanied by a Canada-biased NUANS search report dated not more than ninety (90) days prior to the receipt of the articles by the Director. On request, a number name may be assigned under subsection 11(2) of the Act, without a search.

Item 2
Set out the name of the province or territory within Canada where the registered office is to be situated.

Item 3
Set out the details required by paragraph 6(1)(c) of the Act, including details of the rights, privileges, restrictions and conditions attached to each class of shares. All shares must be without nominal or par value and must comply with the provisions of Part V of the Act.

Item 4
If restrictions are to be placed on the right to transfer shares of the corporation, set out a statement to this effect and the nature of such restrictions.

Item 5
State the number of directors. If cumulative voting is permitted, the number of directors must be invariable; otherwise it is mandatory to specify a minimum and maximum number of directors.

Item 6
If restrictions are to be placed on the business the corporation may carry out, set out the restrictions.

Item 7
Set out any provisions, permitted by the Act or Regulations to be set out in the by-laws of the corporation, that are to form part of the articles, including any pre-emptive rights or cumulative voting provisions.

Item 8
Each incorporator must state his or her name and residential address, and affix his or her signature. If an incorporator is a body corporate, that name shall be the name of the body corporate, the address shall be that of its registered office, and the articles shall be signed by a person authorized by the corporation.

Other Documents
The articles must be accompanied by form 2 'Information Regarding the Registered Office and the Board of Directors'.

Other Notices
If a proposed corporation is to engage in:
a) the construction or operation of a pipeline for the transmission of oil or gas as defined in the National Energy Board Act, or
b) the construction or operation of a commodity pipeline as defined in the Canada Transportation Act,
the incorporator shall inform the Minister of the Department or Agency that regulates such business.

The information you provide in this document is collected under the authority of the Canada Business Corporations Act and will be stored in personal information bank number CCA/P-PU-063. Personal information that you provide is protected under the provisions of the Privacy Act. However, public disclosure pursuant to section 266 of the Canada Business Corporations Act is permitted under the Privacy Act.

The completed documents and fees payable to the Receiver General for Canada are to be sent to:

The Director, Canada Business Corporations Act
Jean Edmonds Tower, South
9th Floor
365 Laurier Ave. West
Ottawa, Ontario
K1A 0C8
or by facsimile at: (613) 941-0999
Inquiries: 1-866-333-5556

Généralités
Si vous désirez obtenir de plus amples informations afin de compléter le formulaire 1, veuillez consulter le Recueil d'information sur la constitution, l'Énoncé d'octroi des dénominations ou les Lignes directrices pour l'octroi des dénominations.

Vous pouvez déposer le formulaire 1 par l'entremise du Centre de dépôt des formulaires en ligne de Corporations Canada au http://strategis.ic.gc.ca/corporations ou encore envoyer ou télécopier le document complété à l'adresse indiquée au bas de cette page.

Droits payables
Centre de dépôt des formulaires en ligne : 200 $
Par la poste ou télécopieur : 250 $

Rubrique 1
Indiquer une dénomination sociale qui satisfait aux exigences des articles 10 et 12 de la Loi. Les statuts constitutifs doivent être accompagnés d'un rapport de recherche NUANS couvrant le Canada, dont la date remonte à quatre-vingt-dix (90) jours ou moins avant la date de réception des statuts par le directeur. Si un numéro matricule est demandé en guise de dénomination sociale, il peut être assigné, sans recherche préalable, en vertu du paragraphe 11(2) de la Loi.

Rubrique 2
Indiquer le nom de la province ou du territoire au Canada où le siège social se situera.

Rubrique 3
Indiquer les détails requis par l'alinéa 6(1)c) de la Loi, y compris les détails des droits, privilèges, restrictions et conditions attachés à chaque catégorie d'actions. Toutes les actions doivent être sans valeur nominale ni sans valeur au pair et doivent être conformes aux dispositions de la partie V de la Loi.

Rubrique 4
Si le droit de transfert des actions de la société doit être restreint, inclure une déclaration à cet effet et indiquer la nature de ces restrictions.

Rubrique 5
Indiquer le nombre d'administrateurs. Si un vote cumulatif est prévu, ce nombre doit être fixe; autrement, il est obligatoire de spécifier un nombre minimal et maximal d'administrateurs.

Rubrique 6
Si des limites doivent être imposées à l'activité commerciale de la société, les indiquer.

Rubrique 7
Indiquer les dispositions que la Loi ou le règlement permet d'énoncer dans les règlements administratifs de la société et qui doivent faire partie des statuts, y compris les dispositions relatives au vote cumulatif ou aux droits de préemption.

Rubrique 8
Chaque fondateur doit donner son nom, son adresse domiciliaire et apposer sa signature. Si un fondateur est une personne morale, le nom doit être celui de la personne morale, l'adresse doit être celle de son siège social et les statuts doivent être signés par une personne autorisée par la société.

Autre documents
Les statuts doivent être accompagnés du formulaire 2 'Information concernant le siège social et le conseil d'administration'.

Autres avis
Si la société projetée doit effectuer :
a) la construction ou l'exploitation d'un pipeline pour le transport du pétrole ou du gaz tel que défini par la Loi sur l'Office national de l'énergie ou
b) la construction ou l'exploitation d'un productoduc tel que défini par la Loi sur les transports au Canada,
les fondateurs doivent informer le ministre responsable du ministère ou de l'agence qui réglemente ces entreprises.

Les renseignements que vous fournissez dans ce document sont recueillis en vertu de la Loi canadienne sur les sociétés par actions, et seront emmagasinés dans le fichier de renseignements personnels MCC/P-PU-093. Les renseignements personnels que vous fournissez sont protégés par les dispositions de la Loi sur la protection des renseignements personnels. Cependant, la divulgation au public selon les termes de l'article 266 de la Loi canadienne sur les sociétés par actions est permise en vertu de la Loi sur la protection des renseignements personnels.

Les documents complétés et les droits payables au Receveur général du Canada doivent être envoyés au :

Directeur, Loi canadienne sur les sociétés par actions
Tour Jean Edmonds, sud
9ième étage
365, av. Laurier ouest
Ottawa (Ontario)
K1A 0C8
ou par télécopieur : (613) 941-0999
Renseignements : 1-866-333-5556

IC 3419 (2004/12) p.2

Industry Canada   Industrie Canada
Corporations Canada   Corporations Canada

Form 22

Annual Return

(Section 263 of the CBCA)

Corporations must file with Corporations Canada an Annual Return (Form 22) along with the prescribed fee within six months following the end of the corporation's taxation year (section 263 of the *Canada Business Corporations Act* (CBCA)).

INSTRUCTIONS

3 Indicate for which taxation year you are filing as well as the taxation year-end as defined in the *Income Tax Act*. For more information, visit the Canada Revenue Agency (CRA) Web site at **www.cra-arc.gc.ca**. Note that a change to the taxation year-end needs the approval of the CRA.

4 Indicate the date of the last annual meeting or the date of the written resolution in lieu of a meeting, signed by all the shareholders entitled to vote. The resolution must deal with at least the following:
- consideration of the financial statements;
- consideration of the auditor's report (if any);
- appointment of the auditor (shareholders of a non-distributing corporation may resolve not to appoint an auditor);
- election of directors (if applicable).

5 A *non-distributing corporation* is a **private** corporation that is not a reporting issuer under any provincial securities legislation.
A *distributing corporation* is a **public** corporation that is a reporting issuer under provincial securities legislation.

6 Declaration

This form may be signed by any individual who has the relevant knowledge of the corporation and who is authorized by the directors (subsection 262.1(2) of the CBCA).
For example:
- a **director** of the corporation;
- an **authorized officer** of the corporation; or
- an **authorized agent**.

Fees: Online filing, $20; filing by mail or by fax, $40. Fees are payable to the Receiver General for Canada.

---

1 Corporation name

2 Corporation number (as it appears on the certificate)

3 Year of filing

Year   Taxation year-end

4 Date of last annual meeting of shareholders or date of written resolution in lieu of meeting

5 Which of the following boxes meets your situation (check only one item)? Please refer to the instructions for definitions

- [ ] Non-distributing corporation with 50 or fewer shareholders
- [ ] Non-distributing corporation with more than 50 shareholders
- [ ] Distributing corporation

IMPORTANT REMINDER

Change of registered office address?
Complete and file a Change of Registered Office Address (Form 3).

Change of directors or change of address of a current director?
Complete and file a Changes Regarding Directors (Form 6).

These changes can be done electronically, free of charge, via Corporations Canada Online Filing Centre at: http://corporationscanada.ic.gc.ca

General
If you require more information, please visit the Forms, Policies, Fees and Legislation section of our Web site at http://corporationscanada.ic.gc.ca or contact us at (613) 941-9042 or toll-free at 1 866 333-5556.

File documents online:
Corporations Canada Online Filing Centre:
http://corporationscanada.ic.gc.ca

Or send documents by mail:
Director, Corporations Canada
Jean Edmonds Tower South
9th Floor
365 Laurier Ave. West
Ottawa ON K1A 0C8

By Facsimile:
(613) 941-0999

6 Declaration

I hereby certify that I have the relevant knowledge of the corporation, and that I am authorized to sign and submit this form

SIGNATURE

(   )

PRINT NAME   TELEPHONE NUMBER

Note: Misrepresentation constitutes an offence and, on summary conviction, a person is liable to a fine not exceeding $5000 or to imprisonment for a term not exceeding six months or both (subsection 250(1) of the CBCA).

Canada

IC 2580 (2004/11)

Keep Your Sanity and Your Shirt

	Canada Customs and Revenue Agency	Agence des douanes et du revenu du Canada		BN	FOR OFFICE USE ONLY

REQUEST FOR A BUSINESS NUMBER (BN)

Complete this form to apply for a Business Number (BN). If you are a sole proprietor with more than one business, your BN will apply to all your businesses. **All businesses have to complete parts A and F.** For more information, see our pamphlet called *The Business Number and Your Canada Customs and Revenue Agency Accounts.* If you have questions, including where to send this form, call us at 1-800-959-5525.

Note: If your business is in the province of Quebec and you wish to register for GST/HST, do not use this form. Contact the ministère du Revenu du Québec. However, if you wish to register for any of the other three accounts mentioned below, complete the appropriate parts indicated in the following instructions.

- To open a GST/HST account, complete parts A, B, and F.
- To open a payroll deductions account, complete parts A, C, and F.
- To open an import/export account, complete parts A, D and F.
- To open a corporate income tax account, complete parts A, E and F.

Part A – General information

A1 Identification of business (For a corporation, enter the name and address of the head office.)

Name

Operating, trading, or partnership name (if different from the name on the left). If you have more than one business or if your business operates under more than one name, enter the name(s) here. If you need more space, include the information on a separate piece of paper.

Business address (This must be a physical address, not a post office box.) | Postal or zip code

Mailing address (if different from business address) | Postal or zip code

Contact person – Complete this area to identify an employee of your business as your contact person in all matters pertaining to your BN accounts. To identify a person for specific accounts, complete the "Contact Person" lines in Area B1, C1, D1, or E1. To authorize a representative who is not an employee of your business, complete form RC59, *Business Consent Form.* See our pamphlet for more information.

First name | Last name | Title | Telephone number | Fax number

A2 Client ownership type — Language of correspondence ☐ English ☐ French

☐ Individual   If so, are you a sole proprietor? Yes ☐ No ☐   Are you an employer of a domestic? Yes ☐ No ☐

☐ Partnership

☐ Other   Are you incorporated? Yes ☐ No ☐   (All corporations have to provide a copy of the certificate of incorporation or amalgamation.)

Complete this part to provide information for the individual, partner(s), corporate director(s), or officer(s) of your business. If you need more space, include the information on a separate piece of paper.

First name | Last name | Work telephone number | Work fax number
Title | Social insurance number | Home telephone number | Home fax number
First name | Last name | Work telephone number | Work fax number
Title | Social insurance number | Home telephone number | Home fax number

A3 Type of operation Check the box below that best describes your type of operation.

☐ Charity ☐ Union ☐ Association ☐ Financial institution ☐ University/school ☐ Municipal government
☐ Society ☐ Hospital ☐ Non-profit ☐ Religious body ☐ Trust ☐ None of the above

A4 Major commercial activity

Clearly describe your major business activity. Give as much detail as possible in the space provided.

Specify up to three main products that you mine, manufacture, or sell, or services you provide or contract. Also, estimate the percentage of revenue that each product or service represents. | % % %

RC1 E (01)

Canada

A5 | GST/HST information – For more information, see our pamphlet called *The Business Number and Your Canada Customs and Revenue Agency Accounts.*

Do you provide or plan to provide goods or services in Canada or to export outside Canada?   Yes ☐ No ☐

If *no*, you generally cannot register for GST/HST. However, certain businesses may be able to register. See our pamphlet for details.

Are your annual **worldwide** GST/HST taxable sales, including those of any associates, more than $30,000 ($50,000 if you are a public service body)?   Yes ☐ No ☐
If *yes*, you have to register for GST/HST.
Note: Special rules apply to charities and public institutions. See our pamphlet for details.

Do you solicit orders in Canada for prescribed goods to be sent by mail or courier to an address in Canada? Prescribed goods include printed materials such as books, newspapers, periodicals, magazines, and an audio recording that relates to those publications and that accompanies them when they are sent to Canada.   Yes ☐ No ☐

Do you operate a taxi or limousine service?   Yes ☐ No ☐

Are you a non-resident who charges admissions directly to audiences at activities or events in Canada?   Yes ☐ No ☐

If you answer *yes* to either of these questions, you **have** to register for GST/HST, regardless of your revenue.

Do you wish to register voluntarily? By registering voluntarily, you must begin to charge GST/HST and file returns even if your worldwide GST/HST taxable sales are $30,000 or less ($50,000 or less if you are a public service body). See our pamphlet for more information.   Yes ☐ No ☐

Part B – GST/HST account information – Complete B1 to B4 if you need a BN GST/HST account (except for businesses in the province of Quebec.) See our pamphlet for details.

Do you want us to send you GST/HST information?   Yes ☐   No ☐

B1 | GST/HST account identification – Check the box if the information is the same as in Part A1. ☐

Mailing address for GST/HST purposes

c/o   Account name (enter the name under which you carry on business.)

Address

Postal or zip code

Contact person – Complete this area to identify an employee of your business as your contact person in all matters pertaining to your GST/HST account. To authorize a representative who is not an employee of your business, complete form RC59, *Business Consent Form*. See our pamphlet for more information.

First name   Last name   Language of correspondence ☐ English ☐ French

Title   Telephone number ( )   Fax number ( )

B2 | Filing information

Enter your fiscal year-end.
☐☐ Month ☐☐ Day

If you do not provide us with a date, we will enter December 31. If you want to select a fiscal year-end that is not December 31, see our pamphlet for more information.

Enter the effective date of registration for GST/HST purposes.
☐☐☐☐ Year ☐☐ Month ☐☐ Day

See our pamphlet for information about when you need to register for GST/HST.

B3 | Reporting period

Unless you are a charity or a financial institution, we will assign you a reporting period based on your total estimated annual GST/HST taxable sales in Canada (including those of your associates). In the column on the left below, check the box that corresponds to your estimated sales. In certain cases, you may be able to change this assigned reporting period. To do so, check the box in the column on the right below that corresponds to your choice. For more information, see our pamphlet.

Total estimated annual GST/HST taxable sales in Canada (including those of your associates)	Reporting period assigned to you, unless you choose to change it (see next column)	Options		
More than $6,000,000 ☐	Monthly	No options available		
More than $500,000 up to $6,000,000 ☐	Quarterly	☐ Monthly		
$500,000 or less ☐	Annual	☐ Monthly	or	☐ Quarterly
Charities	Annual	☐ Monthly	or	☐ Quarterly
Financial institutions	Annual	☐ Monthly	or	☐ Quarterly

B4 | Type of Operation

04 ☐ Listed financial institution   08 ☐ Non-resident   09 ☐ Taxi or limousine operator   99 ☐ None of these types

Part C
Payroll deductions account information – Complete C1 and C2 if you need a BN payroll deductions account.

C1 | **Payroll deductions account**
Check the box if the information is the same as in Part A1. ☐

Account name

Address

	Postal or zip code

Mailing address for payroll deductions	c/o
	Address
	Postal or zip code

Contact person – Complete this area to identify an employee of your business as your contact person in all matters pertaining to your payroll deductions accounts. To authorize a representative who is not an employee of your business, complete Form RC59, *Business Consent Form*. See our pamphlet for more information.

First name | Last name | Language of correspondence ☐ English ☐ French

Title | Telephone number ( ) | Fax number ( )

Do you want us to send you the New Employers Kit, which includes *Payroll Deductions Tables* and information? Yes ☐ No ☐

C2 | **General information**

a) What type of payment are you making?
☐ Payroll ☐ Registered retirement savings plan
☐ Registered retirement income fund ☐ Other (specify) _____

b) How often will you pay your employees or payees? Please check the pay period(s) that apply.
☐ Daily ☐ Weekly ☐ Bi-weekly ☐ Semi-monthly
☐ Monthly ☐ Annually ☐ Other (specify) _____

c) Will you design your own computer program for payroll purposes? Yes ☐ No ☐ If yes, do you need our payroll formulas? Yes ☐ No ☐

d) Do you want to receive the *Payroll Deductions Tables*? Yes ☐ No ☐
If yes, select one of the following: Paper ☐ Diskette ☐

e) Do you use a payroll service? Yes ☐ No ☐ If yes, which one? (enter name) _____

f) What is the maximum number of employees you expect to have working for you at any time in the next 12 months? _____

g) When will you make the first payment to your employees or payees? | Year Month Day |

h) Duration of business operation Year round ☐ Seasonal ☐
If seasonal, please check month(s) of operation. | J F M A M J J A S O N D |

i) If the business is a corporation, is the corporation a subsidiary or an affiliate of a foreign corporation? Yes ☐ No ☐ If yes, enter country _____

j) Are you a franchisee? Yes ☐ No ☐ If yes, enter the name and country of the franchisor: _____

Part D – Import/export account information

Complete D1 and D2 if you need a BN import/export account for commercial purposes. (You do not need to register for an import/export account for personal importations). Complete a separate form for each branch or division of your corporation that requires an import/export account for commercial purposes.

D1 Import/export account identification — Check the box if the information is the same as in Part A1. ☐

Import/export account name

Address

Postal or zip code

Mailing address (if different from above)
c/o
Address

Postal or zip code

Contact person – Complete this area to identify an employee of your business as your contact person in all matters pertaining to your import/export accounts. To authorize a representative who is not an employee of your business, complete form RC59, *Business Consent Form*. See our pamphlet for more information.

First name Last name Language of correspondence ☐ English ☐ French

Title Telephone number ( ) Fax number ( )

Do you want us to send you import/export account information? Yes ☐ No ☐

D2 Import/export information

Type of account: ☐ Importer ☐ Exporter ☐ Both ☐ Meeting, convention, and incentive travel (MCIT)

If you are applying for an exporter account, you **must** provide all of the following information.

Enter the type of goods you are or will be exporting.

Enter the estimated annual value of goods you are or will be exporting. $ _____

Part E – Corporate income tax account information — Complete E1 if you need a BN corporate income tax account.

E1 Corporate income tax account identification – Check the box if the information is the same as in Part A1. ☐

Mailing address for corporate tax purposes
c/o
Address

Postal or zip code

Contact person – Complete this area to identify an employee of your business as your contact person in all matters pertaining to your corporate tax accounts. To authorize a representative who is not an employee of your business, complete form RC59, *Business Consent Form*. See our pamphlet for more information.

First name Last name Language of correspondence ☐ English ☐ French

Title Telephone number ( ) Fax number ( )

Part F – Certification — All businesses have to complete and sign this part. You can sign this form if you are a sole proprietor, a partner, a corporate director, or an officer or authorized employee of the company. You can also sign it if the Canada Customs and Revenue Agency has on file Form RC59, *Business Consent Form* authorizing you as the company's representative.

I certify that the information given on this form is, to the best of my knowledge, true and complete.

Print your name _____ Signature _____

Title _____ Date ☐☐☐☐ ☐☐ ☐☐ Year Month Day

Printed in Canada

Balance Sheet For A Small Business

Use this worksheet to prepare the balance sheet you will include in your business plan. Yours may have slightly different categories depending on the type of business. Use a similar format to prepare pro forma (projected) balance sheets.

Assets		Liabilities	
Current assets		**Current Liabilities**	
Cash in bank	_____	Accounts payable	
Accounts receivable	_____	Short-term loans	_____
Inventory	_____	Other payments due	
Total current assets	_____	in 12 months	
		Total current liabilities	_____
Fixed assets			
Land	_____	**Long-term liabilities**	
Buildings	_____	Long-term loans	
Less depreciation	_____	(due after 1 year)	
Net land & buildings	_____	Mortgage	_____
		Total long-term liabilities	_____
Equipment	_____		
Less depreciation	_____	**Total liabilities (L)**	_____
Net equipment	_____		
		Owners' equity	
Cars & trucks	_____	Investment	
Less depreciation	_____	Retained earnings	_____
Net cars & trucks	_____		
		Total owners' equity (E)	_____
Total assets (A)	_____	**Total liabilities and**	
		owners' equity	_____
		Total assets equals total liabilities	
		plus owners' equity or A=L+E	

"Investment" represents the amount you and/or your partners or other owners have invested in the business.
"Retained earnings" is the net earnings or profit you have put back into the business.
The total for owners' equity (calculated by deducting total liabilities from total assets) also represents the net worth of your business.

Sample Balance Sheet